STARTING TO COLLECT SERIES

ANTIQUE
GLASS

John Sandon

A superb Webbs' rock crystal service by William Fritsche (see page 145).

STARTING TO COLLECT SERIES

ANTIQUE
GLASS

John Sandon

ANTIQUE COLLECTORS' CLUB

©1999 Antique Collectors' Club
World copyright reserved

ISBN 1 85149 286 0

The right of John Sandon to be identified as author of this work has been asserted by
him in accordance with the Copyright, Designs and Patents Act 1988

British Library Cataloguing-in-Publication Data
A catalogue record for this book is available from the British Library

*The author and publishers acknowledge the help of Phillips, International Fine Art
Auctioneers, who have provided most of the illustrations for this book, either
photographed specially or drawn from their extensive archives.*

Printed in England
by the Antique Collectors' Club Ltd., Woodbridge, Suffolk
on Consort Royal Satin paper
supplied by the Donside Paper Company, Aberdeen, Scotland

The Antique Collectors' Club

The Antique Collectors' Club was formed in 1966 and quickly grew to a five figure membership spread throughout the world. It publishes the only independently run monthly antiques magazine, *Antique Collecting*, which caters for those collectors who are interested in widening their knowledge of antiques, both by greater awareness of quality and by discussion of the factors which influence the price that is likely to be asked. The Antique Collectors' Club pioneered the provision of information on prices for collectors and the magazine still leads in the provision of detailed articles on a variety of subjects.

It was in response to the enormous demand for information on 'what to pay' that the price guide series was introduced in 1968 with the first edition of *The Price Guide to Antique Furniture* (completely revised 1978 and 1989), a book which broke new ground by illustrating the more common types of antique furniture, the sort that collectors could buy in shops and at auctions rather than the rare museum pieces which had previously been used (and still to a large extent are used) to make up the limited amount of illustrations in books published by commercial publishers. Many other price guides have followed, all copiously illustrated, and greatly appreciated by collectors for the valuable information they contain, quite apart from prices. The Price Guide Series heralded the publication of many standard works of reference on art and antiques. *The Dictionary of British Art* (now in six volumes), *The Pictorial Dictionary of British 19th Century Furniture Design, Oak Furniture* and *Early English Clocks* were followed by many deeply researched reference works such as *The Directory of Gold and Silversmiths,* providing new information. Many of these books are now accepted as the standard work of reference on their subject.

The Antique Collectors' Club has widened its list to include books on gardens and architecture. All the Club's publications are available through bookshops world wide and a full catalogue of all these titles is available free of charge from the addresses below.

Club membership, open to all collectors, costs little. Members receive free of charge *Antique Collecting*, the Club's magazine (published ten times a year), which contains well-illustrated articles dealing with the practical aspects of collecting not normally dealt with by magazines. Prices, features of value, investment potential, fakes and forgeries are all given prominence in the magazine.

Among other facilities available to members are private buying and selling facilities and the opportunity to meet other collectors at their local antique collectors' clubs. There are over eighty in Britain and more than a dozen overseas. Members may also buy the Club's publications at special pre-publication prices.

As its motto implies, the Club is an organisation designed to help collectors get the most out of their hobby: it is informal and friendly and gives enormous enjoyment to all concerned.

For Collectors — By Collectors — About Collecting

ANTIQUE COLLECTORS' CLUB
5 Church Street, Woodbridge Suffolk IP12 1DS, UK
Tel: 01394 385501 Fax: 01394 384434
———————— or ————————
Market Street Industrial Park, Wappingers' Falls, NY 12590, USA
Tel: 914 297 0003 Fax: 914 297 0068

Contents

Preface and Acknowledgements

When Frederick IV of Denmark travelled through Europe in 1708-9, he saw how Augustus the Strong displayed his glass collection, and instantly wanted a glass room of his own. In Venice Frederick had purchased and was given a vast assortment of costly glass to add to his acquisitions from the rest of Europe. The glass room he built to house it all still exists in the Rosenborg Palace in Copenhagen, a remarkable treasury indeed. Today, though, collecting glass is no longer the exclusive pastime of princes. Wherever you live, glass is readily available, at prices to suit every pocket.

With so much choice it is essential to plan your collection. My aim with this book is to give practical guidance on all aspects of buying and collecting – what to look for and, most importantly, what pitfalls to avoid. In compiling this advice, I have relied on my twenty-four years of experience working in the glass department of Phillips, the Fine Art auctioneers in London's Bond Street. During this time I have handled many magnificent collections and I have been able to draw on Phillips' precious library for most of the fine illustrations in this book. Phillips has also sold a huge amount of less valuable glass that was rarely illustrated in colour, but I have been anxious to include in this guide the kind of glass that a newcomer could pick up inexpensively. I have therefore taken many of these photographs myself, with guidance from Chris Halton who took other excellent transparencies for me. I now realise how difficult it is to photograph glass and I admire Chris's skills enormously.

Having worked for such a long time as part of a team running Phillips' glass department, I must acknowledge with pride the help I have received from Jo Marshall. Jo instilled in me as a young cataloguer a respect for the beauty of glass. She also taught me the proper way to look at drinking glasses, and thus distinguish the fine from the subordinate. Jo's encouragement and friendship since I joined Phillips in 1975 deserves the most sincere acknowledgement. I also want to thank Keith Baker, former head of Twentieth Century Decorative Arts at Phillips, who gave me much assistance with the Art Nouveau and Modern glass sections of this book. My wife Kris Sandon shares my love of glass and lectures on the great glass artists of the past. Kris has helped in so many different ways that this book has become almost a joint effort and I cannot thank her enough.

As a final thought, I would like to dedicate this book to the memory of my close friend Michael Poulson. Michael and I had so much fun collecting glass together. He taught me to enjoy drinking from fine glass, and to appreciate good design in otherwise humble moulded glass. When I inherited Michael's collection of glass, I also inherited his enthusiasm. Had it not been for Michael's untimely death, we would have written this book together. Instead my thoughts on glass convey many of his ideas, passed on to me during twenty years of friendship.

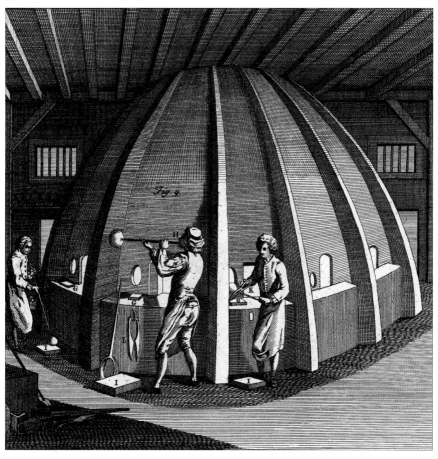

The interior of an 18th century glass house showing glass blowers at work. This print from a manual of 1765 conveniently ignores the evil working conditions that often resulted from the great heat. Sandon collection

Introduction

Mother Nature made the first glass. Obsidian, a product of volcanoes, was used in ancient times to make knives and arrowheads with razor-sharp chipped edges. To manufacture glass, sand is melted in a furnace rather than a volcano, but essentially the material is the same. The techniques of glass-making that slowly evolved in Mesopotamia or Egypt have changed remarkably little over thousands of years.

The science of glass is confusing, for glass is actually classed as a liquid (or more specifically a super-cooled liquid). It is technically a liquid because it is non-crystalline, but of course it appears solid at normal temperatures. To make glass, a source of silicon such as sand or flint is melted into a free-flowing liquid in which other raw materials are mixed. This forms what is known as a 'batch'. To make the manufacture of glass easier, it is necessary to reduce the melting point – the temperature at which the glass begins to flow. This is achieved by adding as a flux-an alkaline material such as potash or soda. At around 1300-1500° Celsius the ingredients fuse together. To aid this fusion a stabiliser such as lime or lead oxide is added, as well as some crushed up broken glass known as 'cullet'. As the mix gently cools and sets, it takes on its non-crystalline form. It is during this cooling phase, halfway between a flowing liquid and a solid mass, that glass can be worked and fashioned into objects of use.

Molten glass, with the consistency of sticky treacle, can either be poured into a mould or blown into a bubble. These two principal techniques were developed in ancient times and essentially have changed little over two millennia. Casting is the oldest process. In Egypt glass hieroglyphics for inlaying or portrait heads of pharaohs were formed in moulds of clay. In Greece a similar technique produced bowls of amber or blue glass that could be smoothed and polished like stone. The 'core-form' method used an internal mould of clay around which thin trails of molten glass were wound. The roughly shaped core was then scraped out to create bottles and jugs for precious unctions.

The discovery of glassblowing was a major advancement that spread through the Roman Empire in the first century BC. To form a vessel by blowing, a 'gather' of molten glass is collected from the crucible on the end of a long tube made of iron. The shape of the gather influences the shape of the blown vessel, and so before air is blown through the tube, the gather is rolled on a flat iron slab known as a 'marvering' table. The bubble, or 'paraison', is inflated by gently blowing through the tube. At the same time, swinging the blowing iron will elongate the paraison. An endless variety of shapes can be made in this way, their forms determined entirely by the skill of the glass-blower. Different tools are used to manipulate the paraison, with tongs and shears to pinch or

The old glass cone at Stuart's factory stands majestically as it has always done. Once a common sight in the Midlands, few of the old cones survive although glass is still made here in the traditional way.

cut the developing vessel and further rolling or marvering to control the shape and surface.

Engravings of traditional glasshouses show that the arrangements inside have also changed little over centuries. The giant brick cones that are so typical of glass manufactories are designed to remove the smoke and channel the air around the central furnace where a draught is directed underneath the fire so that a constant high temperature can be maintained. Within the furnace a series of clay crucibles or 'pots' are arranged in a circle and these contain the 'batch' of molten glass. The pots are replenished in a regular order, so that there is always a supply of melted glass of the correct consistency for the blowers to use. Above each pot is an opening or 'glory hole' through which the glassblowers insert their blowing irons to pick up the gathers.

Glassblowers work in teams of three or four workers known as a 'chair', as traditionally the senior workman or 'gaffer' sat in a specially shaped 'glassmaker's chair' with long flat arms along which careful marvering would take place. A piece of glass would be passed between different members of the 'chair' who in turn would shape the bowl or the foot of the glass being formed. Once the basic shape was constructed, a solid metal rod or 'pontil' was joined to the centre of the vessel so that the other end could be cut from the blowing iron. More delicate finishing and any additional trailed decoration is usually added once it has been joined to the pontil.

Molten glass cools from the moment it leaves the furnace. To keep the glass workable, the partly formed vessel has to be taken back to the furnace and inserted through the glory hole to reheat. When sufficiently malleable once more, the glass can be removed from the heat and blowing and decorating continues.

Roman glassblowers discovered that paraisons could be inserted into clay moulds and blown into predetermined shapes. Wood and metal moulds developed later, and in the nineteenth century the commercial implication of mass-production led to factories churning out identical moulded glass bottles. Machines take the place of glassblowers and identical measures of molten glass are forced into moulds that can be used again and again. Press-moulding, where a blob of molten glass is squeezed between two metal dyes, produces cheap but practical dishes, cups or posy vases, available in different colours. There is an assumption that moulded glass is cheap and inferior to hand blowing, but good moulded glass can be both artistic and infinitely preferable to poorly designed blown glass.

Whatever method is used to form a piece of glass, it cannot be allowed to cool by itself. Different parts of a vessel and different thicknesses of glass cool down and contract at different rates. This causes uneven stress to build up internally, resulting in unstable vessels that can crack or even shatter as soon as they are used. Back in ancient times it was discovered that a carefully controlled, gradual cooling prevented glass objects from cracking. Glass was placed in a separate 'Annealing Chamber' next to the furnace where the heat inside could be reduced very slowly. Annealing tunnels developed through which the cooling glass pieces were slowly drawn until they were further away from the intense heat. Objects can require anything up to sixty hours in the annealing chamber in order to be tough enough to stand regular use. Annealing is an essential part of the manufacture of all glass, including machine-made bottles and windowpanes.

A moulded pattern or any internal ornament is part of the process of forming, but all other decoration is added separately. Trailed glass ornamentation involving molten glass, or additional layers of coloured glass are normally added before annealing, whereas cutting, engraving or any painted decoration is carried out in a separate part of the glassworks well away from the furnace. Internal decoration can range from simple bubbles trapped in a line to intricate patterns of spiral twists in the stem of a wineglass or spread throughout a lavish piece of Venetian *latticinio* glass. In Ancient Egypt mosaic techniques created curious images in coloured glass and these led to Roman *millefiori* bowls that were themselves the inspiration behind Victorian glass paperweights. The Art Nouveau period saw the

The interior of a traditional glass factory in Murano. Above: a gather of glass is formed on the end of a blowing iron in the 'Glory Hole'. Below: glowing white-hot, the gather is taken to the mavering table for forming.

development of many new integral glassmaking techniques including *Pâte de Vere* where the whole piece was constructed using powdered glass of different colours. Many exciting methods of integral decoration, using modern designs and colours, have been used since the 1930s in Scandinavia and in post-war Venice.

Many of the surface decorating techniques practised today go back to Roman times, for the Romans discovered wheel cutting, engraving and enamelling. A rotating wheel of metal or stone will slice a series of facets through the surface of glass with the assistance of lubricating oil and an abrasive powder such as emery. Glasscutters need to be skilled in geometry, for elaborate patterns are marked out on the surface in a series of carefully measured lines. Initial cutting uses a wheel of iron and abrasive sand, followed by smoother stone or wooden wheels and much finer abrasive powders to polish each facet. The wheels are fixed in position while the glasscutters press the vessels to be cut against them. As the glasses are carefully rotated, wonderful sparkling effects are created. Initially hand- or foot-powered treadles drove the wheels. The development of steam-powered wheels led to more accomplished, deeper cutting in the nineteenth century. Today, electric wheels are in general use, while washes of acidic chemicals replace fine abrasives to provide a totally smooth surface.

Tiny revolving copper wheels are used for engraved decoration cut into the surface. Flowers, scenes or inscriptions all rely on the skill of the engraver who sketches the individual design by holding the glass beneath a wheel that is continually fed with oil containing an abrasive. The most detailed engraving uses copper wheels no bigger than a pinhead, while a rather different kind of engraving makes use of the point of a diamond to scratch and stipple a design on the surface of a glass.

Combinations of deep cutting and engraving produce incredible carved effects. In clear glass 'Rock Crystal' engraving resembles similar effects carved into hardstones. When layers of different coloured glass are carved

with fine wheels 'cameo' glass is created. Here, instead of engraved designs cut into the surface (intaglio decoration), cameo glass is created by carving away the background to leave the design raised in relief. The Roman technique of cameo glass was revived in the nineteenth century, particularly in Stourbridge. Cameo glass involves casing a glass vessel with a layer of glass of a different colour. While the Romans carved entirely by hand, in Stourbridge acid was used initially to remove much of the background glass, followed by copper wheel polishing to carve fine detail into the relief. Combinations of acid-resist decoration and wheel polishing created many of the masterpieces of Art Nouveau glass.

Concentrated hydrofluoric acid was also used to etch patterns into the surface of clear glass. To create acid-etched decoration, patterns were firstly incised through coatings of an acid-resistant wax painted on to the surface. The acid cut into the glass where the wax had been scratched away, creating a design etched to an even depth. Acid etching is cheaper than hand engraving, but in spite of this fine etching can still be artistic and of supreme quality.

Layers of different coloured glass are used for many decorating techniques as well as to economise on expensive coloured mixes. A very thin coating or 'flashing' of coloured glass can give a colourless object the appearance of being made of solid red or blue glass for example. When a scene is engraved through a 'ruby-flashed' surface the result is a dramatic coloured background as practised to great effect in nineteenth century Bohemia. A thicker casing of coloured glass is usually referred to as an 'overlay'. By cutting through different overlays, very striking patterns are created when the coloured layers underneath are revealed.

Many different decorative effects can be created by shading glass of different colours. Certain glass is described as heat-sensitive and will change colour at specific temperatures. By heating this glass unevenly at the mouth of the glass furnace, graduated colour can be achieved. Colour can also be applied to the

A selection of working designs for decorative cut glass by John Wadsworth, a freelance designer who adapted Art Deco patterns to suit factory production in England in the 1930s.

surface in the form of stains, while other chemical treatments can recreate the iridescence that forms on ancient glass after centuries of burial. Metallic lustres and rainbow iridescence enjoyed widespread popularity during the Art Nouveau period.

Enamelling and gilding are techniques associated primarily with the decoration of porcelain. Painting is rarely effective on clear glass although some transparent enamels were used most successfully in Biedermeier Vienna. On opaque or coloured glass, however, painted designs and gilding are used in many different ways. Enamels are essentially finely powdered glass mixed with colouring agents. Aided by an added flux, the glass powder melts in an enamelling kiln and fuses the colour to the surface. Gilding requires a lower temperature to fix it to the surface, and can add the finishing touch to decorative glassware, for brightly burnished gold can bestow incredible richness.

Glassmaking is all about teamwork. Great artists such as Kothgasser, Fritsche, Beilby or Kny relied on experienced glassblowers to create the blank goblets or vases on which they practised their engraving or enamelling. The role of the designer is very important as each stage in the manufacture of a fine piece of glass takes careful planning. Successful glassmakers have to understand marketing in order to create work the public wants to buy. Old-fashioned cut glass patterns will not sell alongside more up-to-date designs; while even the cheapest moulded wine bottles require the most complicated planning to create a satisfactory shape and then fashion the machines and the moulds from which they are cast. Since ancient times – from big factories or tiny studios, using mechanised processes or artistry by hand – glass is the most versatile of materials. Golden opportunities lie ahead for all collectors who are indeed spoilt for choice.

CHAPTER 1

Collecting Glass

Beginners are easily bewildered by different prices asked for essentially similar pieces of glass, for the price is determined as much by where you shop as what you buy. With patience and plenty of luck, bargains can be found anywhere, but in order to obtain specific types of glass, most collectors realise they have to go to specialists.

It is nice to think that you can find interesting glass at car boot sales or garage sales, but usually someone has got there first. Initially at a low price, the piece may have passed through an antiques mall or general antiques fair or two before arriving with the specialist, a profit added at every stage. For this reason it is important to 'shop around' and compare prices in order to work out what you should be paying. Some dealers do work on much greater margins than others, and you will always be expected to pay more in the comfortable and convenient surroundings of a selected fair or high street gallery. If you have time to hunt around the bargain shops and flea markets then that's fine – good luck will sometimes come your way. Beyond this, once you start to specialise, the world of auctions and top dealers' exhibitions will beckon and you will need to pay rather more for what you want. It may not be quite as much fun to discover a good piece of glass in a smart antiques shop as in a box of bric-à-brac, but the excitement of the hunt comes with every purchase as your collection grows.

Collections can be small or large, and enormously varied, so it is always important to be focused. It is all too easy to be tempted and to buy any glass you like the look of, and then end up with a meaningless accumulation. A worthwhile collection needs a theme. When I step back and think to myself what attracts different collectors, I realise all glass objects fit into one of five principal groups. These are the reasons why people collect, and pieces bought with a specific aim or purpose ultimately give most enjoyment.

A. Collecting for Use

Most people collect glass for interest and decoration, but it is important to remember that old glass can be very pleasant to use. Every home contains glassware that is used every day. In addition, sets of antique glasses and decanters sit in cupboards in so many houses where the owners are too scared to use them. To me this is almost criminal. I remember once being invited to dinner and being served wine in clumsy tumblers, while in the china cabinet at the side of the room was a cut glass set from the 1930s crowded on a shelf. 'Why don't you use that?' I enquired, only to be told that it was far too precious. It turned out my hostess had paid £6 each for the new tumblers, and she was shocked when I informed her that the sixty year old cut wineglasses were not worth any more than that. For the second bottle of wine we used the old cut wine goblets, and I swear every guest thought the wine tasted better!

Drinking is a pleasure greatly enhanced by a fine utensil. At home I would not dream of drinking out of anything but antique glasses; but this doesn't mean I have had to pay a fortune. All I have had to do is buy single nice Georgian rummers or Victorian cut tumblers. I pick them up in junk shops or in minor antiques fairs and I don't think I have had to pay more than a few pounds for any of them. While I don't mind using odd glasses, sets of old glass still are jolly affordable and remarkable value compared to new. Sets of glass should all match and must contain enough pieces for regular use when you entertain. Often sets are uneven due to breakages, but still contain enough components to be usable. Six is the magic

Collecting for Use. Two very different 19th century drinking glasses. The French tumbler (left) is cut with great precision and every facet is sharp to the touch, while the English tavern rummer (right) was pressed in a two-piece mould and here the facets are rounded and smooth to the touch. In their own way, both are charming to drink out of and, curiously, the value of each is remarkably similar.   Sandon collection

number. Less than six of any size and the set is incomplete. More than six is a bonus and allows for the odd accident. Always avoid wineglasses with chips, though, as nobody likes to be offered a drink in a chipped glass.

Many table services offered for sale contain certain old-fashioned or impractical shapes. Such sets are cheap for good reason. Wine goblets of decent size were used continually and broken, while the silly little liqueur glasses or tiny tumblers always remain. Old sets often contain the flat saucer-shaped champagne glasses while champagne drinkers favour elegant tall flutes today. These days people also like to drink their spirits in nice big tumblers with plenty of room for mixers and ice. Old table sets can be cheap, but add six or more good size wineglasses, champagne flutes or whisky tumblers and the price will escalate.

Decanters are out of favour in today's lifestyles and this is a shame. Hosts like to offer a choice of malt whiskies or different liqueurs and they come in distinctive bottles with re-usable corks. As a result, old decanters are incredibly good value. In olden days many drinks needed decanting and wealthy households paid high prices for suitable serving bottles with tight fitting stoppers. Decanters usually came in pairs or sets of three. Single odd decanters can be used today, of course, but it is rather nice to have a matching pair and the value of a pair is always much greater. When buying decanters for use, make sure the stoppers match in every respect and fit snugly. This prevents evaporation of the contents and staining as a result. Always avoid decanters with their stoppers stuck inside the neck and look carefully for fine cracks, especially in the neck. If the interior of a decanter is cloudy, do not assume it just needs a clean. Years of use literally etch the interior surface and this can only be removed by polishing inside, a costly business left to professionals. Also, when you wash a decanter, let it drain, upside down if possible, and only replace the stopper when the interior is completely dry.

If you are likely to worry or be afraid, then you shouldn't use antique glass. Treat it with care and respect, however, and it will give you a great deal of pleasure.

B. Collecting by Colour, Type or Technique
The individual beauty of coloured glass can be greatly enhanced by forming and displaying a collection. There are endless opportunities to create stunning displays either in a single colour or by careful mixing of different colours and types. Most popular is the choice of a single colour and here, strictly speaking, age is not important. 'Bristol Blue' was made not only in Bristol in Georgian days (see page 94). Bristol is merely a colour and the name is used too loosely. Your collection of blue glass may contain pieces from many countries, some antique and some modern, yet displayed together this really doesn't matter. You should ensure, however, that all pieces are of good quality and a nice even colour. Also, a variety of shapes is usually better than too many pieces all the same.

Cranberry (or pale ruby) glass is another very popular single colour, especially in North America where collections are often displayed on glass shelves in front of a window. In America, fakes of coloured glass abound, unfortunately, but while this does not really matter purely for display, reproductions do not enhance any collection. Similarly, for show purposes damaged pieces of coloured glass can still look fine as part of a colourful display, and will usually cost very little. If possible, though, you should try to buy only perfect pieces as these will generally hold their value better and will certainly give more pleasure.

Collecting a specific type of glass becomes more interesting the more you learn. Victorian 'art glass' is enormously varied. Many pieces are virtuosities of technical excellence, especially satin glass with internal decoration and mother-of-pearl finishes, while English cameo

Collecting by Colour and Type. Three pieces of Victorian cranberry, including a celery vase. Although reproductions are common, it does not take long to learn the true colour and heavy weight of genuine Victorian cranberry glass.

Collecting by Type. Venetian goblets and drinking glasses in traditional style – not precious 17th century originals but decorative 20th century reproductions, made in Murano for display and enjoyment.

glass is even more breathtaking. Cameo glass can also be collected from China and of course from Art Nouveau France, but here you are getting into a very expensive commodity and comprehensive cameo collections can only be formed by well-endowed museums or very wealthy individuals.

Engraved glass encompasses a wide period of history and is available to suit most pockets. When collecting engraved glass it is usually necessary to stick to a specific period, as eighteenth century German goblets do not live happily alongside Swedish shapes from the 1950s. Engraved glass needs to be displayed under very controlled lighting to appreciate the beauty of the decoration, and must always be kept clean and free of unsightly finger marks.

The delicate moulding of American Depression glass also needs good light, but most pressed glass is robust and can be displayed anywhere according to colour or design. Colourless moulded glass is not expensive and early examples can be particularly fascinating. Moulded glass is available in any number of interesting colours, from Hyalith or Lithyalin in the 1840s through to

malachite glass of the 1930s.

Whatever you choose to collect, decide on a type from the outset and stick to it. Milk white glass from Venice, Germany or Staffordshire; Opaline from France in exotic hues; Commemorative glass; Millefiori or Latticinio. There are all sorts of opportunities for a beginner to get started and learn as you go along.

C. Collecting by Shape

An ideal introduction to glass collecting is to hunt out different varieties of a popular object. The scope is enormous, from paperweights to posy vases, decanters to dressing table sets. Here you can be as obsessive as you choose, and set your own collecting criteria, but it is essential to keep a perspective. The shape you select has to be readily available to keep collecting fun, and needs to be priced to suit your pocket. The most important decision is not so much what should you buy as where do you stop. To begin with it is good to buy as many examples as you can and build a worthwhile display; but it can get out of hand.

Bottles are the most popular single shape. Prices for Victorian examples start at about £1

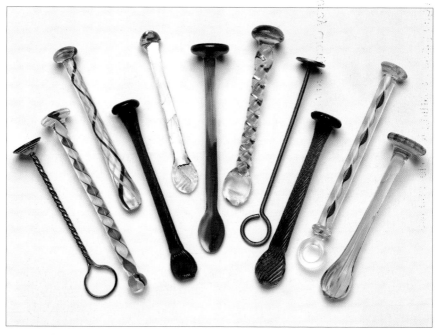

Collecting by Shape. A selection of Victorian glass sugar crushers showing different internal and external decoration. While examples in clear glass are plentiful, coloured sugar crushers are hard to find.

Sandon collection

Collecting by Shape. Three typical late Victorian bottles including a 'Cod' bottle containing a marble, and a poison bottle with a strongly corrugated surface so that the noxious nature of the contents can be recognised at night. Fascinating bottle collections cost surprisingly little.
Sandon collection

Collecting by Shape. The eye-catching beauty of glass paperweights makes them so popular with collectors. These rare antique French examples would be very costly, but plenty of pleasing paperweights are still inexpensive.

each and bottle specialists always have loads to choose from priced at less than £10. I purchased the examples opposite from such a shop selling hundreds of moulded bottles set out according to colour and type. I love to rummage in bottle shops reading the names of long forgotten breweries, patent medicines and mineral waters, and a select number look good in my kitchen. I know some houses where the owner's bottle collections look just like the shop – row after row of pale green and frosty glass in every shape and size. When you can no longer fit any more on to your shelves it's time to have a rethink. Don't buy any more £1 or £2 bottles and go for a smaller number of £20-£40 examples instead, thus upgrading your

collection and weeding out inferior specimens. A drastic cull once in a while is good for any collection. It may not be easy to part with cherished early purchases, but if you can face up to having the occasional clearout, you will end up with a selected and far more appreciative collection.

There are many shapes in glass that benefit greatly from display in quantity. It is wonderful to examine a Chinese snuff bottle up close, but when placed by itself on a sideboard it looks a bit lost. Instead, a collection of snuff bottles, displayed on well-lit glass shelves, can make a wonderful focal point in a room. Similarly, colourful glass paperweights look lonely by themselves, but can be stunning when grouped

Collecting by Shape. Part of the Primrose Orgel collection of Victorian glass flower horns – colourful vases popular around 1850-60. For every kind of glass object, there's always someone somewhere who collects them.

together. For display purposes the maker is generally unimportant, but in any collection quality should be maintained, as inferior specimens do not live too happily alongside the finest available.

Themed collections can mix shapes for variety. Many people in the medical profession collect glass measures, funnels and other medical apparatus ranging from large jars for storing leeches to tiny eyebaths. The perfume business world-wide employs huge numbers and it is hardly surprising that many people whose job it is to sell modern scent or cosmetics choose to collect antique scent bottles or perfume containers. Wine-related antiques are always in demand. Antique decanters take up a lot of space, so large collections are uncommon

and, possibly as a result of this, prices are remarkably reasonable, especially for single decanters. Drinking glasses, on the other hand, are enormously popular. Collectors usually restrict their wineglasses to a specific country and period. Eighteenth century England provides the widest scope and here variety comes in the shapes and patterns of both stems and bowls. Standard forms are relatively easy to come by, but to progress it soon becomes apparent that lots of collectors are all seeking something a bit different, and rare wineglasses will cost a great deal more than common ones. This is true of any single shape you choose to collect, and it always does pay to aim for rarer and better examples as soon as you can extend beyond the beginners' stage.

D. Collecting by Maker, Artist or Place of Manufacture

The most frustrating feature of glass collecting is the general absence of makers' marks. Before the late nineteenth century the presence of any mark or signature is a great exception and, even then, most twentieth century glass is unmarked. As a rule, names only appear on individually made art glass, and certain kinds of ornamental moulded glass where a mark or emblem could be incorporated into a moulded pattern. Once marks become usual on decorative and novelty glassware, it is possible to collect the work of single makers. Some manufacturers were prolific – Sowerby or Lalique for example – and thus plenty of specimens are available within every price range. The work of other individual artists can be somewhat scarce and here collecting can be difficult, especially as rarity usually leads to high prices. Signed pieces by Maurice Marinot, Anton Kothgasser or Fulvio Bianconi are marvellous to own but will cost huge sums, and you need very deep pockets indeed to collect the work of William Beilby or George Woodall.

Glass from named factories is much more available than that from individual artists, and thus you can collect Kosta or Orrefors, Whitefriars or Steuben, even Gallé, Daum and Tiffany. The important rule to follow is always to buy good examples. I believe it is better to collect superior pieces by Meyr's Neffe or Loetz, rather than ordinary or dull Tiffany for the same money. The very best Whitefriars paperweights cost no more than dull, ordinary Clichy or St Louis examples, and a moulded opalescent ornament by Sabino can give more pleasure than a late specimen made after Lalique had lost its sparkle. Display space is all important, too, for you cannot appreciate a collection of Lalique, or Venini, or even older Thomas Webb art glass, unless the lighting is just right. Effective displays should never be crowded.

If you are interested in older glass, it is

Collecting by Place of Manufacture. A selection of Central European enamelled glass, made provincially in regions of Germany, Austria and Bohemia, including a Pasglas *and schnapps flask, 18th century.*

Collecting by Maker. A special collection of English 18th century drinking glasses all decorated in the Beilby workshop in Newcastle. At this level collecting does not come cheaply, but it can be very rewarding.

almost impossible to collect a single maker. Here it is better to go for a regional type or locally made glass, appropriate to where you live or a specific country that interests you. The area around Bristol and Nailsea is linked to all kinds of coloured and novelty glass, and even though similar objects originated in other parts of Britain, many collections have been formed in the Bristol area. Bohemian cut and engraved glass is very popular with collectors in many countries for its colour and quality, and in the United States a great many collectors specialise in American glass. New England glass or other distinctive American types are not understood anywhere outside the United States, whereas collections of Irish glass are international, popular in England, America and Australia, far away from the Emerald Isles where the glass itself originated. Russian glass, Spanish glass – every country has its own distinctive types and very interesting themed collections can be put together.

E. Collecting by Age or Period Style

The period of your home is likely to influence your choice if you collect glass of a specific age. Regency cut glass is difficult to assimilate in a modern home, whereas in a 1960s house, modern design glass from Scandinavia fits perfectly with contemporary furnishings. Strong period design styles never blend easily with one another, and so it is hard to mix Art Nouveau with Art Deco, let alone combine Regency with 1950s, for these are like chalk and cheese. It takes a good eye to tell the precise period of any piece of glass, and in order to learn about a particular era it is essential to study it in isolation. Ancient glass lives comfortably together with early Islamic and Mediaeval, for all tend to be corroded with iridescence. Sixteenth and seventeenth century Venetian glass, however, survives looking new, with most examples hardly conveying an appearance of great age. To be a modest collector of early glass, you do not have to live

Collecting by Age or Period Style. Specimens of Art Nouveau glass tend to be very individual, but it is possible to group together certain types for a distinctive display. These iridescent vases are from Loetz and other Austrian makers, 1900-1910.

in an ancient palace, as you can display old glass on new shelves lit by fluorescent tubes or halogen. Conversely, it is much more difficult to collect modern glass if you live in a really old house, as well-designed glass from the '50s and '60s looks very awkward on dark wood in a panelled interior. Regency cut glass from the early nineteenth century welcomes natural light from dozens of candles but can still sparkle under modern lighting.

Glass has always been the perfect mirror of fashion and it is very satisfying to be able to create an entire period interior, your glass placed on furniture of the same age. You have to decide if you are comfortable living in a museum dedicated to a bygone age, or would you rather mix and match styles of different periods. I feel that, to be effective, a collection should be restricted to a specific time frame where possible, but of course everyone's taste is different. Above all, you must enjoy living with whatever you choose to collect.

ADVICE FOR COLLECTORS

Collecting antiques is a pastime laced with dangers, for fakers have seized every possible opportunity. Sometimes I think glass has more pitfalls than anything else, as fakes and reproductions are only part of the problem. Collectors have to be on guard against cracks and fractures, staining and deterioration, ingenious repairs and repolishing. Learning as much as possible about your subject is essential, and seeking good advice from specialists is a major part of the education process.

A. Buying From a Dealer

The value of the glass you collect determines where you shop, for expensive rarities do not often crop up in junk shops or flea markets. On the other hand, car boot sales are a very productive source for bygone collectables or commercial glass from the 1950s onwards. In Britain boot fairs have become so popular that many are now of enormous size and it can take a considerable time to look around. Getting there early is not as crucial as it used to be, for most traders sell regularly each weekend and their stock has been pretty well picked over. Any decent antiques on sale tend to be at their full value and real bargains are harder and harder to find.

The same is true of the giant flea markets that attract huge numbers of visitors in the United States. Looking around these, I am frequently amazed by the sheer quantity of glass on offer. Many dealers have remarkably similar stock and certain popular collectables appear again and again on different stalls. The prices being asked are also remarkably similar, for everyone has looked up the value in the relevant price guide. If something was for sale at less than the 'list price', the chances are another dealer will have snapped it up before the fair opened and moved it to his or her own booth with an appropriate increase. The result is that dealers have to make do with rather small profits, and in order to form a collection you have very often got to pay the full market price for whatever it is you want. It is still possible to bargain with any dealer to get the price reduced, usually between 10% and 20% off any dealer's ticket. 'The Great Antiques Hunt' and other TV game-shows have encouraged the whole country to expect every dealer to come down in price when asked. A 'Trade Price' used to be just that – a discount given to another antiques dealer, but now everybody wants to barter and dealers have all had to increase their prices first just so that they can come down. It gets a bit silly sometimes when a collector refuses on principal to buy an object they want, solely because the dealer won't come down and give them a 'best price', and believe me this does happen. Because margins are often tight, some sellers cannot afford to reduce their asking price and we should all respect this.

Specialist antiques fairs are taking the place of antiques shops. More and more dealers are giving up costly premises and trading instead from stalls in one-day fairs. Others are moving into Antiques Centres or Malls where they are

likely to attract far more customers than would visit an isolated shop. These centres do offer an awful lot of choice and it is vital to shop around and decide what things you like the most. A lot of dealers specialise in one area, and a dealer selling only glass will attract customers with like interests. One common misconception is the idea that a specialist will always charge more than a general dealer, as frequently the reverse is true. A friendship between a dedicated collector and a specialist dealer guarantees preferential treatment so that pieces known to be of interest are kept back for good customers. Dealers in specific kinds of glass buy a lot of collections privately and sometimes they are able to sell you pieces for less than you would have to pay in competition in an auction room.

Antique glass fairs, or combined ceramics and glass fairs, bring together top dealers in glass from all over the country. These events are well worth a visit as they give you the opportunity to compare prices and to contrast glass of different quality. A cut glass vase may look good in a shop by itself, but in a specialist glass fair you can see others that might be a better colour or have finer cutting. Visit a few fairs and you soon learn what is available within your budget. Specialist glass dealers with their own shops usually have pieces priced for beginners as well as their established clients, and time spent in such a shop can be as much of a treat as a great museum. Most shops are not at all intimidating once you get inside.

Do not be afraid to ask a dealer about the pieces he is selling. Many dealers tend to buy mostly things they know about and often they can give sensible advice to guide you. This is particularly important as far as damage and repolishing is concerned. I discuss the problems of polishing later in this section and I know that a lot of people do get caught out. Most dealers are genuine and sometimes they don't know that a piece they are selling has been cleverly repaired. Your protection here is your receipt. Even if you have no reason to be suspicious, always ask a dealer if the piece you are interested in has had any repolishing. A reputable dealer will be happy to reassure you and will state the condition in writing along with the date of manufacture on his receipt. Never settle for anything less, for your own insurance purposes if for no other reason. If you retain a proper receipt you will have some redress if you discover afterwards that an item you bought is in fact a later copy or has at some time been expertly mended.

B. Buying at Auction

When you buy at auction you do have the protection of the law if your purchase turns out to be not as described, but the situation is not always clear-cut. More private collectors are now buying at auction themselves, and television shows such as 'The Great Antiques Hunt' and 'The Antiques Show' portray salerooms as accessible and friendly places, fun rather than threatening. There is tremendous excitement spotting something you want during a sale preview and wondering whether your bid will be successful. Some people get a great thrill from bidding in person in a sale, while others find it daunting and prefer to ask the auctioneer's clerk or a porter to bid for them. This means deciding your limit before the auction and this is usually a good thing, as in the tense atmosphere of a sale it is all too easy to get carried away and bid higher than you intended. If you are not used to auctions it can be nerve-wracking, wondering if your bid will be seen or if you might buy the wrong lot, but in practice an experienced auctioneer very rarely if ever misses a bid. The key is to bid clearly with an obvious wave until the auctioneer has seen you.

Most auctions publish printed catalogues giving a brief description and usually an estimate or guide price. The quality of the catalogue as well as the expertise behind it will vary greatly. A major auctioneer in London or New York will produce a profusely illustrated work of reference that is usually reliable in every respect. You cannot expect a provincial or regional saleroom to have the same experience, and descriptions in the catalogue of a country auctioneer should be taken only as an approximate guide unless you know the staff responsible have specialist knowledge.

The author conducting a sale of glass at Phillips in Bond Street. Attending a specialised sale is always an excitement, particularly for the auctioneer as the prices go up and up.

Consumer protection legislation means that you have redress if items bought in any auction turn out to be not as described, but in practice buyers in dispute often have a tough battle to get reimbursed by some smaller auction firms. Nevertheless, you should always keep your receipt together with a copy of the auction catalogue.

Unless you are sure of what you are bidding on, don't ever be afraid to ask questions of the auction staff. Preferably ask to speak to the specialist who catalogued the lot as he can often provide useful background information about a particular piece. If the staff seem cagey and unwilling to talk about a piece, be suspicious. Some auctioneers list damage in their catalogues, either in detail or with the symbol 'AF', but never assume all damage is going to be noted. One cataloguer may regard small chips to a piece of glass as too trivial to mention, but to a specialist collector these chips may be crucial. In my London sales I indicate all visible damage such as chips or cracks, but I do not attempt to define any repolishing that might have taken place, as this can be such a controversial area. I find it very hard to state categorically that any piece has never been repolished. Rather than attempt to list cut-down rims or polished-out chips in the catalogue, I prefer instead to discuss any piece with potential buyers individually, to alleviate their fears or else to agree that a repair might have been carried out at some time in the past. Once again, you cannot expect a cataloguer in a small auction room to recognise a very clever repair, just as a general dealer is also likely to be unaware of certain professional restoration that may have been carried out.

Most auctions charge a buyers' premium – a commission paid by the purchaser – usually of an extra 10% to 15% plus VAT or sales tax. This covers the costs of running the auction business and in return buyers are able to rely on a regular supply of specialist antiques gathered together in one place. In a London saleroom an auction might have more than a hundred lots of eighteenth century drinking glasses, or good Art Nouveau and Twentieth Century Designer pieces, thus presenting as much choice as the combined stock of a great many antiques shops or fairs that would take ages to visit. Buyers' premiums are now commonplace and it is very easy to take them for granted – but never forget the extra you have to pay when deciding the limit of your bids.

C. Buying over the Internet

On-line auctions via the Internet are a rapidly expanding phenomenon. At the same time it is possible to browse through the stock of antiques dealers thousands of miles away from the comfort of your home computer. Shopping in this way can become compulsive, but I find downloaded photographs of glass rarely convey an accurate feel of the actual piece. The colour of glass, in particular, is very hard to judge from a digital image on your screen. Buying at auction is not straightforward. The process of continually increasing your bid in an Internet auction can be a frustration, and

whether you are successful in the end can depend purely on the time the final bid is received. All the same, a vast number of glass objects are now auctioned in this way and traditional collectors must be prepared to embrace the new technology. Descriptions posted on the Internet do tend to over-glamorise mundane objects and there is no opportunity to feel for chips or signs of repolishing.

Virtual Antiques malls can be an interesting way to learn the price dealers charge for pieces in different locations and different countries. If you find a piece of glass you like on a dealer's Web page, rather than clicking the 'buy' button, I strongly recommend a telephone call or e-mail to the owner asking for more information and some reassurance as to condition. This also gives a chance to negotiate on the price. Postage and insurance costs can add quite a bit to an Internet purchase. Insurance is essential, as it is apparent that many sellers are not experienced in packing delicate items of glass so that they survive the mail service intact. Finally, don't forget customs regulations can apply duty and VAT to many pieces mailed from abroad.

However and wherever you choose to buy, collecting glass should always be enjoyable. Select pieces with which you feel happy, set yourself a budget and within this always buy the best that you can afford – a few good objects instead of a lot of ordinary ones. This way you can soon build up a worthwhile collection that gives you pleasure. I promise that once you have caught the collecting bug you'll never stop having fun.

D. Damage and Repair

Part of the magic of glass is its fragile vulnerability, for once broken its desirability evaporates. Costly pieces were repaired in antiquity, for even Egyptian tombs have yielded pieces of glass crudely mended with metal rivets. Elizabethan silver collars and bands held together the snapped stems of precious Venetian goblets, while broken feet were replaced with rings of turned wood in which the stem could be imbedded. Really old repairs can be quite fascinating, but most of the value was destroyed the moment the glass broke. No matter how well it is mended, a damaged glass will never be worth anything like that of a perfect piece. This is why clever modern repairs are such a problem to the collector.

Most cracks and breaks are easy to see. A piece of glass that has been badly broken can be stuck together again, but it will only be of interest if it was sufficiently rare to begin with. Archaeological relics can still be worth owning if discovered in pieces and reassembled, and an important object, such as the broken armorial goblet by William Beilby (illustrated on page 48) is still worth a considerable sum. Aside from unique specimens, however, broken glass should be avoided.

Just a very fine crack will devastate a glass's value, so before you buy any piece, take time to examine it more than closely. Hold it to the light and look out for irregular refractions. Bottles or decanters can be 'dunted' and develop a bruise or 'star-crack' in the side, while stress over the years can cause cracks to develop near the pontil beneath a glass. The most common place to find a crack, however, is at the base of any handle, for pressure here can be considerable. When a jug has cracked right at the base of a handle where it joins the body, it can be very hard to see. A crack can often be felt with a fingernail, but the best way to detect such a fault is to 'ring' the glass with your finger. Tap the handle softly as you balance the piece carefully, and a good piece will ping nicely. A crack will usually result in a 'clunk' sort of sound. Some cracked glass will still ring true, but this simple test can prevent many costly mistakes. Needless to say, you should never pick up a piece of glass by the handle without first checking for any cracks. If a handle comes away in your hands, you will find it very hard to convince the owner or dealer that it must have been cracked beforehand.

Obviously glass chips easily. Sometimes a chip will not break away and remains as a 'bruise' which can be seen when caught in a certain light. Glass paperweights are very prone to bruising. Specialists use a formula based on the circumference of a bruise to calculate how deep it penetrates, in order to decide if it is possible to polish the damage away. Any piece of glass can be polished to get rid of chips and if done by a professional this can be very difficult to detect. You have to remember that a lot of glass, when it was made, was finished off by polishing to leave the rim even and smooth. Bohemian beakers, for example, usually had slightly chamfered rims cut on a polishing wheel, while the tops of cameo glass vases were usually polished to remove the uneven edge of the overlay. The problem facing all collectors is to decide whether a rim shows original polishing from when it was made, or has it been chipped and cut down later.

The most common repolishing is to the rim or foot of a wineglass. A glass grinder will remove any unsightly chips so that a set of glasses can continue to be used. A small, shallow rim chip can be buffed and polished smooth, but as a result the rim of the glass will be thinner at the point where the chip has been removed and you should look for evidence of this. The foot of a wineglass should be perfectly circular. If it appears irregular or elliptical, even, this probably means that the foot has been trimmed at one side (see the illustration on page 31). To avoid irregularity, many glass polishers remove an even amount of glass from the entire circumference. This affects the proportions of the glass, and a foot that has been 'cut down' usually looks too small. The process of trimming the foot of a wineglass removes any tool marks left on the rim during manufacture and any wear or rubbing that might have built up over two centuries. A repolished foot can also feel sharp rather than naturally rounded at the edge. A high-power magnifying glass will assist, but do look closely, and always be on your guard as in most instances repolishing has a serious effect on the value of a piece of glass.

There is, of course, no limit to the amount of glass that can be cut away to remove signs of damage. An object can be completely altered in this way and I have seen repairs that are most ingenious. Broken decanters can be cut down to make finger bowls or coasters. Wine goblets without stems become stirrup cups, and a broken vase cut in half can become a dish or ashtray. Modernist and Art Nouveau vases were sometimes made in irregular shapes, and consequently damaged specimens that have been re-cut into new rather curious forms can still look very convincing. Unwary collectors have been known to pay substantial sums for basically incomplete broken vases that have been 'doctored' by clever repolishing.

Taking repairs a stage further, two broken pieces can be joined together to make one apparently perfect object. A wineglass with a broken foot can be cut off cleanly at the base of the stem. This can then be glued on to another foot that has been cut off a different glass. Modern super-glues and epoxy resins can accomplish joins without any evidence of the adhesive showing. Likewise I have seen decanters with replacement necks, or stoppers where the 'stem' of the stopper has been recreated and joined invisibly. For generations glass repairers have been providing a valuable service mending chipped and broken family sets, so that services of table glass can continue in use. Once such sets are sold, however, a cosmetic repair made with the best of intentions can suddenly become a hidden danger to an unwary collector.

Ancient glass has often been the subject of ingenious restoration, where the neck or handle of one vessel has been attached to the body of another. Even the Portland Vase was repaired centuries ago using for the base a disc of cameo glass in place of the original pointed foot. Glass items that have been expertly 'restuck' can be very hard to detect. Ultraviolet light is a valuable tool, as the chemical make-up of different pieces of glass will fluoresce different colours. The separate components forming a repaired Roman glass specimen will often fluoresce differently and give the game away. Some adhesives will also glow under ultraviolet light and reveal otherwise invisible repairs, while a light can help show up areas where resin has been used to re-fill chips to coloured glass. Lightweight portable ultra-violet lamps are now available from the home security sections of DIY or hardware stores and are not expensive. For many collectors,

such a lamp could represent a wise investment.

All collectors need to be worried about repairs to glass, but thankfully this is not nearly as big a problem as that faced by collectors of pottery and porcelain, as really invisible repairs are impossible in a material you can see right through. The important things to remember are always to ask before you buy and to take a close look yourself. Keep your eyes open, but do not be afraid, as this will take the fun out of glass collecting.

E. Fakes and Forgeries

In the eighteenth century, visitors taking the 'Grand Tour' were offered all manner of antiquities to take home as souvenirs. There were not enough genuine marble busts to go around and so copies were carved to order. Glass presented dealers with a problem, as the skills used in ancient times to make the most desirable coloured and mosaic effects had mostly been forgotten since the third century AD.

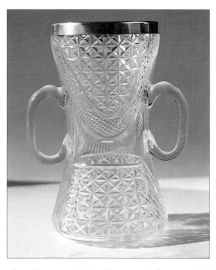

The silver mounts date this vase to the year 1900 and it is cut glass rather than moulded. In its day, however, it was a commercial piece, lacking the excitement of cut glass made in the Regency period. Such pieces today are unfashionable and consequently inexpensive.

The foot of this wine glass had been chipped at some time and has been re-polished. The foot is now uneven with clear evidence of the original damage. The value is naturally affected.

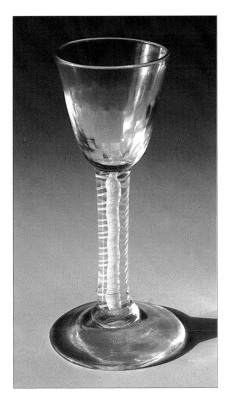

Glassblowers in Venice were encouraged to reinvent the methods of gold sandwich glass, mosaic and cameo, and their copies of ancient glass were sold to dealers who buried them on archaeological sites to await the next visit by unsuspecting wealthy tourists.

As interest in collecting antiques spread worldwide in the mid-nineteenth century, the faking of valuable glass increased to supply the new demand. Old Venetian glass was fetching enormous sums, while some of the factories that made the originals were still working using the same formulae and local sand. Commentators noted that some of the new Venetian glass shown at the 1851 Great Exhibition was precisely like the treasured mediaeval originals. In due course Salviati's reproductions were bought by Victorian collectors to use every day or to display in their

mock Elizabethan homes for a fraction of the cost of the real thing. More than a century later, without maker's marks or identifying labels, *vetro à reticello* and *vetro à retorti* glass (see Chapter 4) can be terribly difficult to date. Experts sometimes fail to agree, so what hope is there for the beginner? Much as it is nice to dream of making a valuable discovery, if a piece of ancient coloured glass or any fine Venetian glass is offered to you without provenance, you have to assume it is a nineteenth century copy or else you are taking a very big gamble.

By the early twentieth century, every kind of old glass was keenly collected and I think it is safe to say that there is not a single area that has not attracted the attention of the forger. Bohemian *Humpen,* Dutch *Roemers,* English balusters and airtwists, Regency cut glass, Biedermeier beakers, you name it, someone has copied it. John Northwood copied Roman cameo glass while Louis Comfort Tiffany copied the iridescent surface of ancient glass, but while we do not regard their masterful creations as fakes, their own fine art glass has been much imitated. Without the need to reproduce the appearance of age, Art Nouveau, Art Deco and Modernist glass has been faked extensively in recent times. Even the 1950s and '60s Venetian creations such as glass clowns and fish vases were copied at the time

'Suzanne', an opalescent sculpture by René Lalique and a contemporary 1930s copy probably from Czechoslovakia. The cheap version was not made to deceive, for it would have been sold in an everyday glass shop rather than an expensive gallery selling Lalique. Sometimes, however, fake Lalique marks have been added later to Commercial Art Deco figures to try to catch the unwary.

in Czechoslovakia and the Far East. Forgers today encompass the very latest technology, even using irradiation chemically to change the colour of genuine pieces of Lalique glass. I cannot possibly list every kind of fake that you are likely to come across, but just as a taster of what went on I will mention just a couple of the most frequently encountered deceptions.

English drinking glasses were considered superior in the eighteenth century and were exported extensively, especially to Scandinavia and The Netherlands. Customers familiar with the streaky lightweight soda glass made in Holland much preferred to use the heavier, clear lead glass of England. Dutch glass factories copied English glasses in the mid-to-late eighteenth century, reproducing the shapes and stems of English airtwists and opaque twists. Copies of English 'Jacobite' engraving were executed on bell-shaped bowls, and highly desirable colour twist stems were much reproduced. Some Dutch glassmakers are now known to have used lead glass, while in

Norway a glassworks at Nostetangen made many English style wineglasses, particularly balustroid stems in lead glass of a noticeably dark colour. These contemporary copies of English drinking glasses have two centuries of natural wear under the feet and often come with long family histories as provenance. The quality, though, is usually inferior to fine English glass and a Dutch colour twist with a messy red spiral stem deserves to be worth only a fraction of the original English version.

By the end of the nineteenth century, when collectors were paying high prices for early glasses, various outright fakes were made. Many were sold as sets to customers living in old-fashioned houses who wanted to drink out of antique style glass. Thomas Webb and other English firms made reproduction glasses using a brilliant clear lead glass that generally looks too good to be true. Feet are often flat and lack pontils, and stems tend to taper (thicker at one end), while many are far too big for the kind of glass they are copying. Some, though, with facet

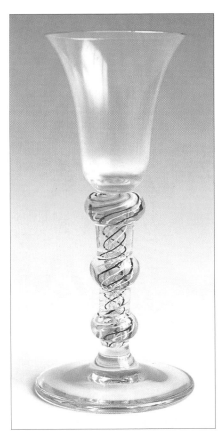

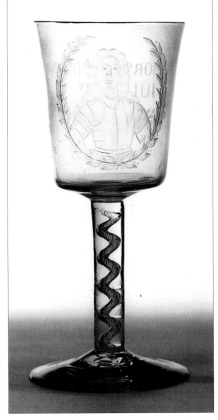

A triple-knopped stem is rare on any opaque twist stem wine glass, and coupled with a multicolour twist this would be a very great rarity indeed. In fact the glass used for the bell bowl is too bright and clear, the foot is too flat, and the quality of the twist is disappointing. This was probably made around 1920.

This 18th century wine glass depicts George Walker, a little-known supporter of William III and a rare subject to find on a Williamite glass. Sadly, while the glass is authentic with provenance from an old Irish family, the engraving was added much later, and is probably the work of Franz Tieze who faked engraved glasses in Ireland in the 19th century.

cut stems and engraved birds or chinoiserie scenes, frequently sell to the unwary as genuine.

A different kind of deception involves perfectly genuine wineglasses that have been altered. It is of course possible to add engraving to a glass at any time. Some baluster wineglasses had Jacobite engraving added twenty to fifty years later, while the stipple engraver Laurence Whistler sometimes used glasses that were two centuries old. The problem comes when much later engraving purports to be original. Franz Tieze, a skilled engraver from Bohemia, worked in Ireland in the mid-nineteenth century making clever copies of Williamite and Jacobite engravings, using wineglasses that were originally plain.

No doubt he wasn't the only engraver to indulge in this lucrative trade, and recently huge doubts have been cast on a great deal of valuable engraved glass. That such doubts are justified can be shown by some obviously fake large airtwist stem glasses made in the 1910s and '20s that carry very convincing Jacobite engraving. If the same engravers had used eighteenth century glasses instead of modern copies, their work would probably be accepted without question. A most worrying state of affairs thus exists where experts are divided and collectors with very expensive specimens have their heads filled with doubts.

The last thing I want to do is discourage new collectors from the exciting world of eighteenth century drinking glasses just because of the preponderance of fakes. Every corner of the art market is riddled with reproductions and spurious glasses stand alongside all kind of other fake antiques and collectables. Indeed, I do not know of recent fake wineglasses, for engraved airtwists or convincing balusters are just too darn difficult to make. Instead the current trend is for the fakers to concentrate on Art Nouveau iridescent and cameo glass and moulded Art Deco.

When top names in Art Nouveau started to command huge sums, inexperienced collectors were caught out left, right and centre by forgers who didn't even have to make their own glass. Instead famous names were added to inferior

A 'Roman' glass bottle probably made in the Middle East in the 1960s. Copies of ancient glass are everywhere and most aim to fool only naïve tourists. This piece has been artificially 'aged' and was still joined on to the blowing iron when dipped in acid. Consequently, when the pontil was snapped off, the scar in the centre of the base remained shiny and free of the acid-induced deterioration. Over 1600 years of genuine burial would have left the pontil mark equally covered with iridescence.

A two-light table candelabrum in the Regency taste, purporting to date from early in the 19th century. Instead the glass is too brilliant and the proportions are incorrect. An examination of the metal fittings shows these are also of the wrong age. This was probably made in the 1950s.

specimens. Iridescent glass by WMF or Meyr's Neffe and by many smaller unknown makers looked vaguely like Tiffany or Loetz. A dentist's drill added 'L.C.Tiffany Favrile' to all kinds of cheaper Edwardian art glass and these were eagerly snapped up by beginners who knew the names but hadn't handled the genuine quality of the real thing. Similarly the name of Lalique was added to every kind of art deco moulded vase. This fraud was often so blatant that gamblers who parted with their money almost deserved to get stung. Fakes of Gallé were more difficult as an old piece of cameo glass was needed and a polishing wheel or acid to cut in a new signature. Unmarked 1900s cameo glass had the embossed names of Gallé or Daum added where a leaf or some other part of the design had once been. I have, for example seen pieces of old Beijing (Peking) cameo glass with added 'Gallé' marks, and in one instance an authentic Chinese jade cup was 'signed' to turn it into a rare Daum ornament in Oriental taste.

Technology eventually overtook the belief that fine Gallé cameo cannot be faked because no one has the skill to execute it. Today in the Far East and in Eastern Europe unbelievable amounts of Gallé vases and lamps are produced alongside Tiffany leaded glass lampshades. The Gallé pieces are made using many layers of coloured glass with deeply etched cameo surfaces. Ambitious floral and landscape designs shimmer when lit from within just like the real thing. Of course the quality does not approach the real Art Nouveau glass of Gallé and his contemporaries, but it looks good and sells in quantity worldwide. I have seen recently the same pieces selling in New York, Athens and Gdansk, and so I realise that the more I travel, the more I am going to see. The cameo work on the fake pieces is generally sharp to the touch with acid etching to a very even depth, and the interiors are usually spotlessly clean for something supposedly made up to a century ago. Many modern Gallé pieces include the letters 'TIP' concealed in the design in an attempt by their makers to pass them off as reproductions rather than fakes. However, loads of vases get brought along to the Antiques Roadshow by

Although this recent fake copies a commercial Gallé cameo glass vase, it still lacks the spirit of Art Nouveau that makes the real thing so desirable. The leafy branches are stiff and lifeless and the layers of cameo are somewhat thin. Fake Gallé vases are being made today in enormous numbers and a great many people are taken in by them.

members of the public who have been completely fooled, even though they have parted with between £40 and £200 for pieces that ought to have cost thousands.

This is the key, of course. No antiques dealer is going to sell a genuine Gallé vase for £80, whether in an Athens flea market or a Sunday antiques fair or through an auction of Victoriana and bric-à-brac. Thankfully most

These monumental vases are in the manner of overlay glass made in Bohemia in the mid-19th century for the Middle Eastern market, but these are reproductions, apparently made in Eastern Europe no more than ten years ago. While lacking the quality of the almost priceless real thing, they are still a tour de force *of glass-making and are highly decorative. 38in. (97cm) high.*

people realise that, at the price they are being asked, something must be wrong. If you don't know your Gallé glass, you should buy only from an established specialist dealer or top auction room with their reputations as your guarantee. Now that more and more fakes are being created, of every kind of antique, you must always go around with your eyes wide open. Be cynical and suspect everything, but don't be so afraid that collecting is no longer a pleasure. Common sense is usually all you need, and never be ashamed to ask questions.

CHAPTER 2

What is available within your price range

UNDER £20 ($30)

The Children's Antiques Roadshow is a special BBC programme once a year where young people bring along their collections. Amongst the Dinky cars, Star Wars toys and stamp collections we are used to seeing more and more glass as this area is now appealing to a new generation of collectors. The most popular kind of pocket money collection formed by children is glass animals, for these are plentiful and above all cheap. From these inexpensive novelties children learn to respect the fragility of glass, as all their collection must be treated with care. Age does not matter (unless you come across rare eighteenth century Nevers glass animals). Instead the key is to find a well-made piece rather than an amateur effort from the end of a seaside pier. The best glass animals today originate in China.

Glass bottles are widely available for just a couple of pounds. As I discussed in Chapter 1, collections of shapes that are so readily available can get out of hand, and it is wise to specialise in a particular kind of bottle – mineral water, coloured poison bottles and so on. With plenty of room, a display of Victorian bottles can be surprisingly decorative. There are numerous books and magazines about bottle collecting, and keen collectors join clubs and go digging for their own bottles in Victorian refuse tips. Medicine bottles appeal to doctors and other members of the medical profession, for there is plenty of scope within this price range, including eye baths, feeding bottles, measuring tumblers and other

Under £20. Miniature glass animals are the ideal starting point for young collectors and rarely cost more than a few pounds. Look out for examples that are well made, such as this modern Venetian duck by A . Scarpa.
Sandon collection

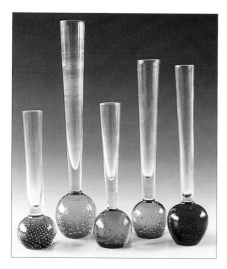

Under £20. Bud vases with beaded bases to display a single flower. These were very popular in the 1960s and '70s and form a cheap and colourful collection for £2 to £5 each.   Sandon collection

Under £20. Medical glass has a wide following among collectors. Victorian funnels can be beautifully made and are usually cheap.

Under £20. Colour-printed tumblers from the 1950s and '60s, good examples of modern design for just a pound or two. Also fun to use.   Sandon collection

Under £20. Glass costume jewellery is enjoying a great revival. This Art Deco buckle and cut glass beads, some with an iridescent sheen, date from the 1920s and '30s. Look out for finely cut examples.

Sandon collection

graduated measures and laboratory equipment such as funnels. Devotion to a single shape can be rewarding, as in the case of sugar crushers (see page 20), but always go for variety rather than quantity, as duplicates serve no purpose in a growing collection.

A great deal of very usable glass costs less than £20 ($30). Cut glass is not expensive, but moulded plates, dishes and cake stands, particularly in colourless glass, cost very little and can be used as well as displayed. The older drinking glasses that can be bought for £10-£20 ($15-$30) tend to be small, crude and plain and it is better to pay more for better single glasses. An exception is the colourful decorated tumblers that were so popular from the 1950s onwards. Great designs from the 1960s are presently neglected, while cartoon subjects, from Tin Tin to Toy Story, offer enormous potential as they now find their way into car boot fairs. Amongst the best value in boot fairs and charity shops is glass jewellery. Cut glass beads cost a great deal when bought from modern factories in Scandinavia as each has to be individually cut by hand. Strings of old coloured beads from the 1920s and '30s can be

picked up for a fraction of the modern price, but values have been rising fast now that costume jewellery is enjoying a revival. A glass collection that is wearable has obvious appeal. Look for good quality plated mounts, for old jewellery looks cheap if the poorly stamped metal fittings are corroded and dull.

£20-£50 ($30-$75)

Drinking glasses are so plentiful that it is important to decide your price range and aim for good examples. At less than £50 ($75) you should avoid damaged or stained specimens and choose well-made glasses reflecting the period in which they were made. Eighteenth century glasses will cost too much, but Regency or early Victorian glasses are readily available. Plain blown or moulded rummers are hard to find in sets, but pleasing single rummers are functional and also look good displayed on shelves. Similarly, jelly glasses or other serving shapes like patty pans, and some simple ale glasses from the eighteenth century can all be found within this price range.

Moulded glass comes into its own above

£20-£50. 'Tear Flasks' and Unguentaria *in Roman glass from the 3rd-4th century AD. With characteristic iridescence, at £30-£50 each it is quite extraordinary that something this old can be bought for so little.* Sandon collection

£20-£50. Eye baths in different shapes and colours form an interesting collection, from as little as £5-£8 for a late moulded specimen or up to about £50 for a 19th century blown glass example.

£30 ($45). Look out for pleasing examples of American Depression glass, some carnival glass and English pressed glass in amber or pale blue. Pieces can have commemorative interest, and much of it reflects period design as even cheap commercial glass changed when

£20-£50. There is enormous scope in the field of drinking glasses for less than £50 and it pays to specialise. These small wines from the early 19th century are 'deceptive', the thick bowls suggesting they hold more than they do.

£20-£50. Patty pans (or tart pans) in English glass from the mid- to late 18th century. Individually blown and often with folded rims, these little dishes were used for pâté, custard or pickles. 2¾in.-3⅜in. (7cm-8.5cm).

Michael Poulson collection

Art Nouveau and Art Deco in turn replaced Classical and Gothic. Fine antique paperweights are very expensive, but pretty examples don't have to cost a fortune. Scottish, Czechoslovakian and the better Chinese weights offer good scope as serious paperweight collectors often ignore them. Advertising paperweights were popular in America early this century and can be fascinating. Smart design in glass from the Post Second World War period is a growing market and it is worth hunting junk markets for 1950s and '60s ashtrays. As these can now cost up to £50 ($75) each, it seems absurd that a Roman unguentarium (or tear flask) from the fourth century AD can be bought for under £40 ($60). In reality so many have been dug up they are actually quite common.

£50-£l00. When you use nice glasses, it doesn't matter if they do not match. You can form a 'Harlequin' set such as this from different overlay hock glasses from England and Czechoslovakia, c.1890-1920.

£50-£100. Single decanters offer enormous scope for the beginning collector. Many gorgeous Victorian examples, and some of Regency date, can be bought for well under £100. Make sure the stoppers are original, and avoid interiors that are stained.

£50-£100 ($75-$150)

Throughout this book I advocate using old glass for the pleasure it gives to drink out of something that is well made. Dining habits have changed and we don't entertain today as lavishly as our parents and grandparents. Every part of a meal once had its own utensil but much of the specifically designed glassware lies unloved in the back of a cupboard. Finger

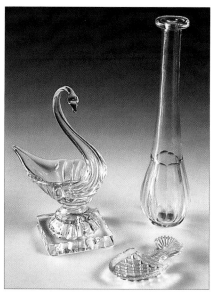

£50-£100. Brilliant cut glass is generally out of fashion. Pre-1930s examples can usually be bought for a great deal less than new vases in department stores. Look out for quality and avoid any pieces with chips.

£100-£250. Interesting shapes in Regency and early Victorian glass can be expensive, but they make collecting enjoyable. Left: a blown swan salt with 'lemon squeezer' base. Above: a 'toddy lifter' for serving punch. Front: a cut glass caddy spoon.

Sandon collection

bowls or wine coolers (used to chill or rinse wineglasses on the table) are no longer used, but nice Georgian and Victorian examples are relatively inexpensive. A pleasing single decanter – Regency or early Victorian – will generally cost less than a new cut glass decanter and this doesn't make a lot of sense. Collections of decanters take up a lot of room and from a practical point of view small or half-size examples are the most reasonable. Cruet bottles – often looking like miniature decanters – can be even better value. Single dishes from dessert sets, or parts of silver épergnes long melted down, show the skills of the old glass cutters and display beautifully if clean and with only minor chipping.

In this price range some eighteenth century glasses are affordable but with generally unexciting plain stems, though they do show their colour well. Nineteenth century glasses are better value here, for colour and decoration combine together to present enormous scope. Deep green or amethyst wineglasses from the first half of the nineteenth century are usually nicely shaped. Later Victorian glasses costing up to £100 ($150) each are beautifully decorated with careful cutting. Bohemian glass tumblers in clear or coloured glass can also cost less than £100 but avoid poor workmanship and concentrate instead on good design.

£100-£250 ($150-$375)

Victorian and early twentieth century art glass has fallen from favour in the past two decades, partly due to the profusion of fakes. The result of this is most reasonable prices for some of the best examples. It is now possible to buy attractive baskets or posy holders in 'Vaseline', Burmese or 'Peachblow' for between £100 and

£100-£250. Glass scent bottles attract a great many enthusiasts for they form a colourful collection that does not take up a lot of room. Prices start from a few pounds, but in this price range better quality cut glass examples can be found.

£150 ($150-$250). Cranberry glass is a very popular single colour and for display a variety of shapes is always preferable. Similarly, a collection of so-called 'Bristol Blue' can be dramatic (see page 94). If you are paying over £100 ($150) for single pieces, it is imperative to avoid damage unless an item is particularly fine or rare. Decorated art glass such as Mother O'Pearl Satin should never be bought if it is bruised as repairs are impossible.

Above £100 ($150) each, wineglass collectors can now afford to buy eighteenth century

£100-£250. Chinese snuff bottles are collected all over the world. Glass bottles with interior paintings are particularly charming although many on the market now are not particularly old.

£100-£250. The wonderful colours of 19th century English glass look spectacular when brightly lit. Forever associated with the name of Bristol, coloured glass was actually made all over the country.

45

examples with airtwist or opaque twist stems, as well as light balusters, some sweetmeat glasses and engraved ales or jellies. In Regency glass attractive shapes are available, ranging from cream piggins to novelties such as toddy lifters. All sorts of novelties in the 'Nailsea' style are readily available, from top hats, bugles and walking sticks to ships under glass domes. Collections of Nailsea can be difficult to display, but if you have got the room they can look magnificent.

Within this price band you will not find serious Art Nouveau glass or good Art Deco by makers such as Lalique, but you can find plenty of well-designed glass in the same fashion by minor makers. I always believe that an ornament that has been well made to a good design, by a maker you may not have heard of, is still preferable to a poor commercial example by a better-known name.

£250-£500 ($375-$750)

When spending upwards of £250 ($375) on a piece of glass, the maker becomes important and it is worthwhile seeking signed pieces.

Within this price range it is possible to find only relatively ordinary pieces of Lalique, Gallé or Webbs, but rather better pieces can be acquired by smaller, little-known makers. Good Bohemian or Scottish paperweights rather than ordinary Clichy or Baccarat. Nice Scandinavian art glass by Kosta or Orrefors in engraved clear glass comes in most attractive shapes, or for £250-£300 ($375-$450) you can buy the very top range moulded glass. Victorian cut glass water jugs, engraved glass jugs and decanters, matching pairs of antique decanters – there is immense scope. In eighteenth century drinking glasses you can now afford good twist stems with interesting shaped bowls; while in the nineteenth century you can use matching sets of wines or cut tumblers. Continental beakers will be well engraved or colourful, and some nice overlay glass is well within this range. This is the price of good plain onion-shaped bottles or sealed cylinder wine bottles, while a great deal of interesting Roman and Islamic glass costs less than £500 ($750). With the exception of antiquities, where repair may be acceptable, when you are spending this kind of money on

£250-£500. Collecting glass with a specific local theme can be rewarding. These 19th century rummers all depict the bridge over the river Wear at Sunderland and were popular souvenirs for visiting ships' captains.

£250-£500. Early English vernacular glass is robust and can have considerable charm when displayed on old oak furniture. These jugs, dating from the early 19th century, are usually attributed to Nailsea or Wrockwardine (in Shropshire), although they were also made in many other regions.

a single piece of glass, it is imperative to buy perfect specimens wherever possible. Chipped or polished pieces will inevitably prove difficult to sell should the need arise.

MORE THAN £500 ($750)

'Buy the best you can afford' is a message drummed into me since I was little, and there is no denying that expensive pieces do generally remain in demand and rise in value at a greater rate than anything that is mundane. Of course spending large sums on single delicate glass objects does involve risk and many collectors would be too scared to own such pieces. You cannot be a collector if your possessions frighten you. Naturally you should always take precautions to protect such valuable items. Place your pieces in a display cabinet rather than leave them sitting out in the open in a vulnerable position, and of course make regular checks to ensure the shelves in your cabinet are secure. Adequate insurance cover is vital.

Without worry, you can then enjoy ownership of some really wonderful glass. To hold its investment potential, valuable glass needs either age (combined with rarity), impeccable workmanship or the name of a top artist or designer. Without these factors be very careful when asked to spend a high sum on a single piece. Of course all is relative. £1,000 ($1,500) will buy a very good piece of English art glass but a rather more ordinary piece of Gallé or Tiffany. English cameo glass is much more expensive than Beijing glass of similar age and workmanship, and a wine bottle made in 1670 will cost you much, much more than one made in 1710. It is very important to learn about your subject first. Attend several auctions without buying a thing, just to learn the prices; or ask several dealers to recommend pieces to you before deciding what to buy. Firm attributions are imperative, for a piece of soda glass believed to come from the England of George Ravenscroft will command a far higher sum than a related piece that is felt to be Dutch.

Over £500. In the field of English drinking glasses, the sky's the limit when rarity is concerned. A little twist of colour multiplies the value of an opaque twist stem at least fifteen or twenty fold, while enamelling by the Beilbys also sees prices escalate. This armorial goblet by William Beilby, celebrating the marriage of William V of Orange in 1767, is badly broken in the bowl, but still has a value of several thousand pounds. The goblet 7¼in. (18.5cm).

Over £500. Bohemian and Viennese glasses in the Biedermeier taste are highly collectable. These relatively simple examples, from the workshops of Anton Kothgasser and Carl von Scheidt, are painted in subtle transparent enamels and are valued between £1,000 and £3,000 each. 1825-1840. 4in. to 5⅜in. (10.5cm. to 13.5cm).

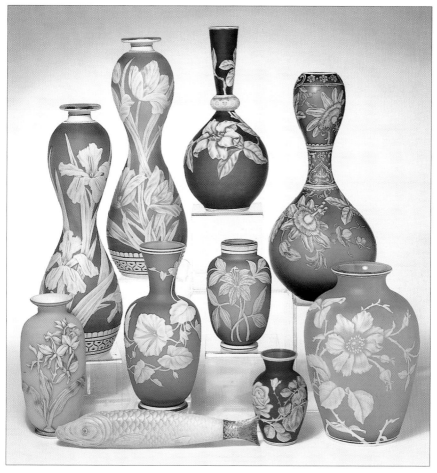

Over £500. English cameo glass from the great Stourbridge makers around 1880-90. The strong shapes and powerful designs work well together and with powerful lighting any collection looks dramatic.

Buy only pieces you find attractive and are happy to live with, as instant profits rarely materialise. Above all, remember the importance of condition. Serious collectors are seriously fussy. They measure the height of a Lalique car mascot to within half a millimetre to ensure it has not had a chip polished out, and a tiny bubble trapped beneath the leaf of a Clichy flower paperweight can make a difference of several thousand pounds. In the upper echelons of any collecting field, very subtle variations can lead to a huge price difference. With glass the sky really is your limit (the present auction record stands at just over £2.3 million); but remember that if something is enormously rare, it will be very hard to put together a collection of similar pieces. Just buy what you are comfortable with, and enjoy it.

CHAPTER 3

Glass in the Ancient World

Most histories of glass begin with the mythical account, recorded by Pliny, of how a group of merchants once camped beside the river Belus in Syria. They placed their cooking pots on the sand raised up on part of the cargo they were transporting – cakes of natron, a rich source of soda. In the morning they found that the sand and the soda had fused together, creating the first ever glass. The real invention of glass was probably a bit more scientific, but the effect would have been much the same. This is likely to have occurred in Mesopotamia around five thousand years ago. Potters had discovered that glazes could be added to the surface of bricks of clay to add colour to buildings, and also to provide decorative coatings on vessels and other precious ornaments. The primitive glazes, which were made of coloured glass, could be used on their own to mould small inlays or beads. Early in the second millennium BC it was realised that if glaze was applied around a core, and the core then removed, a vessel of glass could be created.

It is uncertain where the core-formed technique was first employed – Mesopotamia or Egypt – but it is likely to have been invented around 1650 BC. We know, however, that it was in use in Egypt during the New Kingdom for vessels have been discovered bearing the royal seal of Tuthmosis III who ruled Egypt in the fifteenth century BC. Moulded glass was used for making amulets and beads, as well as inlays, the best of which were finely polished. The treasures discovered in the tomb of Tutankhamun included many pieces inlaid with coloured glass, such as the celebrated golden throne. Glassmaking flourished in Egypt where there was an abundance of sand, extensive natural lakes of natron and in those days no shortage of trees for fuel.

The principal method employed was to create on the end of a metal rod a core of clay roughly formed into shape. This was dipped several times into a crucible of molten glass, usually dark blue in colour. The rough vessel could be decorated by trailing with threads of coloured glass paste in rings or zigzags. These were smoothed on the surface by marvering or rolling the vessel on a flat surface. Handles or rims could then be added, and when cool the interior rod was removed and the clay core was picked away.

Four main types of vessel were created in Egypt using the core-formed process. The *alabastron* was a cigar-shape bottle with a rounded end used to contain cosmetics and some have survived still with their contents and fine spatulas inside. The *aryballos* was similar but with a round body, while *amphorae* had pointed bases and swelling bodies, usually with twin handles. The *oenochoe* was a small ewer or jug with a trailed handle and spreading foot on which it could stand upright. Other vase shapes were made and even delightful perfume flasks in the shape of fish or birds. The trailed or feathered outer decoration was applied in bright colours, particularly yellow, pale blue and red. Most surviving examples have been found in Egyptian tombs where, thanks to the dry climate, they have been preserved in perfect condition. Needless to say, however, clever fakes abound, understandable in view of the high cost authentic specimens now command.

These core-formed vessels enjoyed enormous popularity and continued to be made virtually unchanged for something like fifteen centuries. Precise dating is difficult, especially as the technique was revived in the Hellenistic Greek Empire with very little variation. Methods of glassmaking had been brought to the Eastern Mediterranean in the late Bronze Age and vessels resembling Egyptian forms were made in Syria, Palestine, Crete and Cyprus. Continual wars in the region led to the decline of most ancient arts, and glassmaking, as a luxury industry, was almost wiped out.

Resurgence occurred in Phoenicia and Assyria in the eighth century BC, when bowls and cups were made of translucent glass which was cast in moulds and then polished. Decoration was restricted to simple wheel-cut lines or other limited engraved ornament. Blocks of solid glass were turned on lathes or carved, rather like carving stone, using tools of quartz or flint which were harder than glass. The core-formed process was re-employed and from the seventh century BC beads and pendants were made in the shape of tiny bearded male heads. These have great charm, but again genuine examples are today very costly.

Glassmaking was introduced to Italy in the eighth and seventh centuries BC, but the centre of the industry remained in the Eastern Mediterranean. From the sixth to the fourth centuries BC core-formed vessels were made at Mycenae and other parts of the Greek Hellenistic Empire, closely resembling Egyptian types but created using greater care and fine control of applied feather patterns. Hellenistic glass is famous today for its cast vessels made from the fourth to the first century BC of a clean, translucent material which was beautifully polished and available in several colours including blue and purple. The molten glass was poured into clay moulds and in Greek one word used for glass is 'poured stone'. The best pieces were finished off after casting by highly skilled gem cutters.

Some Hellenistic glass was painted and gilded, and this led to the invention of 'gold sandwich glass' whereby designs in gold leaf were applied between two clear glass vessels of identical shape which were then fused together using heat. Another major invention from Egypt or the Eastern Mediterranean in the first centuries BC was mosaic glass, where pieces or 'canes' of patterned coloured glass were built up on a core and melted together, revealing delicate internal patterns when the

A Greek core-formed alabastron *in dark blue glass with characteristic zigzag trailing feathered on the surface in different colours. This originally contained cosmetics and would have been used with a bronze spatula. c.5th-4th century BC. 5½in. (14cm).*

51

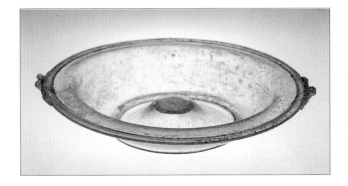

A Roman dish or shallow bowl in almost colourless pale green glass, two serpent-like trails applied as ornament to the rim. c.1st century AD. 6⅞in. (17.5cm) diameter.
Sandon collection

A Roman pale green glass bottle-shaped flask or vase, the surface simply cut on a wheel with bands of close grooves. c.2nd century AD. 6¼in. (16cm). Sandon collection

surface was polished. The finest bowls had trailed rims formed of tiny coloured spirals, and in some cases gold was included in the mosaic glass patterns. Such pieces had great value in the ancient world and today these can only been seen in museums. It is a treat to marvel at such pieces in great national collections for, apart from some simple core-formed objects, it is unrealistic for ordinary collectors to contemplate owning pre-Roman glass.

The Roman Empire brought with it a unification of arts and cultures stretching from the Near East to the whole of Europe and the Western Mediterranean. Strong communication and trading links meant that glass produced in the distant provinces of Syria, Alexandria and Palestine were exported to Rome itself and from there to all of Roman Europe. Domestic glassware found at archaeological sites from North Africa to Russia exhibits a uniformity in style and decoration, with the result that the majority of pieces cannot be ascribed to any specific place of manufacture. Roman glass is surprisingly plentiful, due to mass production following the invention of the techniques of blowing and blown-moulding.

The first use of blowing molten glass

Three typical shapes in Roman glass. Left: a double balsamarium *with elaborate trailing, c.4th century. Centre: a 'Janus' head flask mould-blown in pale aubergine, 1st~2nd century. Right: an olive green jug with trailed neck, 3rd-4th century. 5⅞in. (15cm) high.*

occurred probably at Sidon in Syria in the middle of the first century BC. Sidonian glassblowers, such as the famous Ennion who signed some of his moulds, moved to Rome in the second half of the first century BC. By the time of the birth of Christ quite superb glass was being manufactured in Alexandria and Sidon in the East and in Italy in the West. Many migrant workers from Egypt and Syria settled in the Western Empire, establishing factories for the making of domestic glass in the Rhone valley in Gaul, in Germany, Belgium and possibly Britain. By the end of the first century AD the Rhineland glass industry centred at Cologne had grown to rival Sidon and Alexandria. Cemeteries linked to the Roman garrisons based on the Rhine have yielded numerous fine large cinerary urns of almost clear glass. Similar sizeable storage jars were widely used alongside thin domestic glass of all kinds, the

quality always surprisingly high.

The most extraordinary thing about Roman glass is the huge quantity that survives. Rarities of course will cost a lot of money, but it is perfectly possible to form a representative collection on a modest budget. The most readily available items are *unguentaria* – phials, bottles and ewers for cosmetics and the scented oils used at communal baths. Unbroken 'tear bottles' – simple tear-shaped blown glass flasks – can be found for as little as £30-£40 ($45-$60), while even the larger and very elegant 'Candlestick Unguentaria' rarely cost more than £200 ($300). Ideal beginners' pieces, the reality is these shapes are commonly encountered. Of course, serious collectors aspire to something more unusual and there is plenty of Roman glass that is quite remarkable.

The use of moulds was widespread in the first century AD. Square-section bottles with

A Roman squat shaped bottle with simple pinched ornament, the olive green glass showing character-istic iridescence. 3rd~4th century. 2¾in. (7cm) high.
formerly Leonard Bernstein collection

A Roman cone beaker from the Eastern Mediterranean, in pale green ornamented with grape motifs and blobs applied in dark blue glass. Elegant cone shapes originated as lamps and developed into drinking vessels in the late Roman period. 4th-5th century. 7⅝in. (19.5cm).
Sandon collection

single trailed handles are relatively common as the shape was strong and has survived well. Distinctive moulded shapes include flasks in the shape of dates or bunches of grapes, in green, yellow or purple. Others take the form of human heads, including the famous 'Janus Head' flasks that have two faces back to back, so-called after the Roman God. Exceptional moulded vessels were occasionally signed by the mould-maker and the names of Ennion, Aresteas and others are now legendary. Coloured glass beakers were moulded with figures and it is possible some of these with circus scenes or gladiators in combat were given as prizes at athletic games.

During the second and third centuries AD clear, colourless glass, perfected at Sidon and Alexandria, was popularly used and new techniques were developed to decorate vessels. Roman glassworkers practised almost all of the main technical processes used today. Cutting using a revolving wheel of flint created patterns of geometric shapes, ovals and faceting polished on the surface of delicate clear glass. Figure subjects and stories from mythology were cut in *intaglio* into bowls and cups, while other scenes were engraved often with careful attention to detail. The most incredible examples of glass carving date from the end of the first century BC and the first century AD. Cameo glass involved a layer of white glass overlaid on to deep blue and carved back to leave a pattern in relief. The celebrated Portland Vase is one of the most important treasures in the British Museum and the word priceless is an understatement. Masterpieces of ancient carved glass are rarely offered for sale and cause much excitement. I watched in awe in December 1997 when the Constable Maxwell diatreta was sold at Sotheby's for the British Rail Pension Fund. This remarkable cage cup, created in the third century AD and a triumph of the lost technique of ancient glass reticulation, sold for more than £2m. This stands as a record price for any piece of glass although it lies firmly outside the scope of this book.

Because of the size and nature of the Roman Empire, some centres of glassmaking declined and secrets were lost, while new processes were developed elsewhere. The quality of moulded glass deteriorated after the first century AD and the art of cameo was forgotten. Instead during the third and fourth centuries greater use was made of trailed and applied decoration, often in a different colour glass. Fine threading was created by allowing a single strand of trailed glass to wind around the neck of a vessel as it spun on a lathe, a technique which continued into Frankish and Saxon glass. Enamelling – painted in colours on the surface – was used for the first time in the third century, and at the same time the technique known as *fondi d'oro* or gold sandwich glass was reintroduced, a revival of the process used in Hellenistic days six centuries earlier. *Latticinio* decoration, using spirals of white patterned tubes inlaid into clear vessels, was one of several processes used by the Romans and then forgotten until rediscovered in Venice in the Renaissance a thousand years later.

The end of the Roman Empire saw rule transfer from Italy to Constantinople in the East where Byzantine traditions were established. Here glassmaking was encouraged and a wide range of vessels was made at Sidon and Tyre in Syria. The shapes were generally debased versions of later Roman forms using naturally coloured greenish glass with occasional blue trailing. From the fifth century, however, Christian symbols were used to decorate the moulded flasks and bottles that now held Holy Water rather than scented oils. Gold sandwich glass had a new important role as tiny mosaic shapes were created for the walls and interiors of the domes of the new basilicas.

In Central Europe the Romans were driven back by Barbarian invaders. The Germanic tribes, generally known as Franks, continued many aspects of Roman civilisation but there

was a noticeable reduction in glassmaking. Far fewer shapes were made and decoration was mostly limited to trailing and the occasional use of inlaid white threads. Soda was still used in the manufacture, but Frankish glass was less pure than the Romans had made and many tiny bubbles can be seen trapped in the mix.

Very different Teutonic drinking customs determined the shapes that were made. It was considered inappropriate for a guest to place an empty glass down on a table, and instead it would be taken away and refilled. Drinking horns and slender 'cone beakers' were made with pointed ends, and some have remarkably fine trailed decoration. Other pouch-shaped beakers or 'palm cups' were made with round bases designed to be held in the hand. Frankish glass from the fifth to the eighth century has been discovered in Germany, Britain and Scandinavia but it is believed the main production centre was in the area of present-day Belgium. The most famous examples of

A Roman or Frankish pouch-shaped bottle in amber glass with very fine trailing typical of some later Roman productions, c.5th-6th century. 4⅛in. (10.5cm). Sandon collection

Teutonic glassmaking are the *russelbechers* or 'claw beakers', decorative vessels which have applied trunk-like claws applied around the sides. Several fine examples have been excavated in Anglo-Saxon sites in southern England, but these are only to be seen in museums, for Frankish and Saxon glass is enormously rare. Even less glass has survived from the Dark Ages of the eighth to the twelfth centuries, for Christianity forbade the placing of ritual offerings in graves and glass chalices were also banned from church use. Instead glassmakers turned their attention to making window glass as the fashion for stained glass spread across Europe. Meanwhile alchemists slowly developed the science of medicine and called for phials, retorts and glass specimen bottles.

Far more exciting developments had taken place in the Islamic world. During the fifth century Sassanian Persians made wonderful use of cutting to decorate clear glass vessels, especially on bowls which have cut circles standing out as raised bosses. Examples which have survived in the dry climate of Iran and Mesopotamia have mostly developed a golden iridescence of quite remarkable beauty. As the Arabic followers of Mohammed drove out what remained of the Roman and Byzantine culture, new kinds of domestic glass emerged to suit different customs. Trailed glass flasks resemble later Roman *balsamaria* but these were placed on the backs of glass camels to form the celebrated 'dromedary flasks'. Pincered decoration was now used as well as forms of stamped ornament. Islamic glassmaking was centred in Baghdad and Basra

Left: an Islamic sprinkler flask known as an ommom *in wafer-thin glass, the long neck designed to prevent the contents from evaporating. c.10th century. 5¾in. (14.5cm). Right: a Sassanian 'Molar Flask' thickly cast and wheel cut with deep facets. c.7th century. 2in. (5cm). This also would originally have had a long neck.*
Sandon collection

from the middle of the eighth century where thickly cast and cut scent glass were made alongside mould blown sprinkler bottles for perfume. Most vessels were given long necks to prevent evaporation in the arid climate of the Middle East.

The decoration of Islamic glass was closely linked to religion, as lamps and sprinkler flasks were made for use in mosques. Surface decoration, whether cut by a diamond point or a carving wheel, matched illuminated texts from holy books with calligraphy as ornament. Wheel cutting became ever more skilful from the ninth century, particularly in Northern Iran and Nishapur. By the eleventh and twelfth centuries carving culminated in the so-called 'Hedwig' beakers. Often mistaken for rock crystal and indeed in many ways finer, these are believed to be Egyptian but were exported all over Europe and prized as holy relics.

Islamic glassmakers revived cameo and mosaic techniques and introduced enamelling and the use of lustre. Gilding was applied within the glass once more, and gold leaf formed the background to calligraphic text from the Koran on precious Syrian mosque lamps. These wonderful creations of the thirteenth and fourteenth centuries allowed the Word of God to shine out with an awesome glow, as their light was reflected by walls lined with Isnik pottery tiles. Enamelled glass beakers were taken by returning Crusaders as far away as Britain, while other trade routes took Syrian glass to the court of the Emperor of China. An invasion by Mongols, however, led to the capture of Damascus in 1400 and brought to an end the dominance of Islamic glassmakers. Although there was a revival in Shiraz two centuries later, by this time Venice had captured the lead.

An elegant Islamic sprinkler bottle in almost colourless glass with heavy iridescence caused by burial, thinly mould-blown with a band of 'eye' motifs on the shoulder. c.11th century. 10¼in. (26cm).

Sandon collection

Further reading

Constable-Maxwell Collection of Ancient Glass, Sotheby's Auction Catalogue, 1979

Sidney M. Goldstein, *Pre Roman and Early Roman Glass in the Corning Museum of Glass,* New York 1979

D.F. Grose, *Early Ancient Glass in the Toledo Museum of Art,* 1989

D.B. Harden et al., *Glass of the Caesars,* British Museum/Corning Museum of Glass/ Romisch-Germanisches Museum, 1987

Marilyn Jenkins, *Islamic Glass, A Brief History,* New York 1986

J. Kröger, *Nishapur – Glass of the Early Islamic Period,* Metropolitan Museum of Art, New York 1995

This Venetian sprinkler flask was valued highly in the 16th century so that when the slender neck broke, mounts of gilded silver were added instead. The striped decoration, or Vetro à fili, *is rare in these colours.*

CHAPTER 4

Mediaeval Europe and the Dominance of Venice

From Constantinople to Greece, the golden domes of Byzantine basilicas shimmered under the glow of saintly images portrayed larger than life in incredible glass mosaics. Meanwhile, as the power and influence of the Catholic Church extended across Europe in the twelfth century, new windows of colourful stained glass illuminated the much-enlarged cathedrals. In this way ecclesiastical wealth supported many glassmakers, even though chalices of glass were forbidden in churches, as they were considered inferior to precious metals. In Europe generally unimaginative domestic glass typified the Dark Ages. Consequently wealthy merchants and princes treasured the rare imports of Byzantine glass and enamelled and gilded Islamic beakers.

By the thirteenth century Venice had emerged as a major sea power and forcibly replaced the Islam States as the centre of trade between the East and the West. The powerful Doges of Venice were presented with valuable gifts from the Middle East and some of these still survive in the Treasury of St Marks, displayed alongside relics brought back by Crusaders following the fall of Constantinople in 1204. These treasures include masterpieces of Roman and Syrian glass (including a Roman diatreta). In mediaeval Venice this glassware was proudly displayed and represented great wealth. Venetian merchants were inspired and they brought other glass goods back from Syria and Damascus to sell on at a profit throughout Europe. They realised fortunes would be created if similar glass could be manufactured locally, and consequently in the thirteenth century Venice began to make its own glass à la façon de Syrie including enamelled beakers.

The Venetian glass industry grew rapidly and was strongly controlled with restrictions even on which months of the year glassmaking was permitted. Furnaces were established throughout the city, and it was to prevent a serious risk of fire that in 1292 all glass factories were forced to move from Venice to the nearby island of Murano. The city authorities feared glassworkers would take their valuable skills to other cities and so, although skilled makers were finely rewarded, all were prevented on pain of death from leaving Murano. Understandably Venice kept its monopoly and as a result very little glass was made elsewhere in Italy. Yet in spite of armed guards, some workers did manage to escape and, enticed by promises of great wealth, established factories in many other European countries making glass à la façon de Venise. Venetian glass skills were no longer secret, especially after 1612 when Antonio Neri published in Florence his 'Art of Glass' (L'Arte Vetraria), a detailed handbook describing many difficult processes.

All forms of fine and applied arts flourished in Italy during the Renaissance. Rivalry between rich patrons encouraged the glassmakers to experiment with new processes, new colours and exciting new shapes and decoration. From the fifteenth century mirrors were perhaps the most valuable productions, made possible by the very even, clear soda glass now made in Venice. This colourless glass was called by the Venetians cristallo because they claimed it was as clear as the mineral rock crystal, a name which has led to much confusion ever since. In reality the early Venetian cristallo was far from perfect, containing bubbles, streaks and specks of impurities, but it was still a great improvement on the Forest glass made elsewhere in Europe.

Beautiful coloured glass goblets and bowls were made in Murano from the late fourteenth century, especially in translucent purple, blue

Venetian style or façon de Venise *wine glasses with distinctive serpent stems, possibly from the Netherlands, the left-hand goblet with diamond-point engraving, the right-hand example in 'Ice Glass'. Glasses like this have survived because they were treasured as too costly to use. All early 17th century. 6¼in.-7in. (16cm-18cm).*

and a bright opaque turquoise. Following the decline of Islamic glassmaking, particularly when Constantinople fell to the Turks in 1453, further Eastern glassworkers came to Venice and introduced the processes of enamelling and gilding. The Venice school of painting was reflected in portraits applied in opaque enamels to coloured glass, often on a gold ground. Magnificent betrothal goblets were painted with scenes within borders of fish-scales and other formal patterns, which mirrored contemporary maiolica, while dots of white and coloured enamels simulated applied gems. Armorial decoration became popular, in particular the Lion of St Mark, one of the emblems of Venice. By 1500 a pure white glass had been perfected which naturally resembled porcelain. Known as *lattimo,* or milk glass, this was used for some of the finest painting, for example a vase with a portrait of Henry VII of England, which is now in the British Museum.

Coloured glass became less fashionable in the sixteenth century as the quality of *cristallo* continually improved. This almost colourless glass was exceptionally thin and light and was skilfully formed into drinking goblets.

Ornament was concentrated on the stems, which were delicately trailed in clear or in blue glass with twisted loops known as 'serpent

A plate of Venetian 'Cristallo' glass with diamond-point engraved decoration of roses and flowers. It is not completely colourless and contains some imperfections, but around 1600 it was a precious commodity. 9¼in. (23.5cm.) diameter.

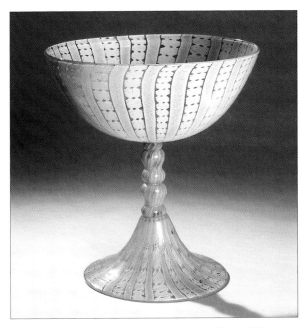

A beautiful stemmed goblet in vetro à retorti, *with detailed internal lacework. Glass of this type was made in Venice from the end of the 16th century into the 18th century, and so precise dating is difficult.*

stems'. The bowls could be patterned with subtle flutes or honeycomb, or else made from a new textured 'ice glass' formed by cooling the molten glass rapidly in water and so creating the pattern of cracked ice which is also known as *cracquelé*. Engraved decoration gained popularity now that diamonds were available from India. Diamond point engraved glass or *vetri intagiate* was mostly limited to floral themes. Wheel engraving was not used to any great extent because the glass was so thin. Merchants complained of many costly breakages caused by the fragility, a significant factor as Venetian glass was widely exported. Trade with the Middle East was now in reverse, as mosque lamps and sprinkler bottles with tall necks were made in Venice for the Islamic market.

In the sixteenth century Venetians developed new colours to imitate valuable polished agate and other hardstones, especially turquoise and *calcedino,* a delicate marbled glass in tones of brown and olive green, which imitated chalcedony. Gold dust was suspended in glass to imitate aventurine, and *lattimo* or milk glass was enamelled to copy Chinese porcelain. The pure white glass was combined with *cristallo* in incredible patterns known as *latticino,* which brought new fame to Venetian glass.

Filigree glass was first recorded in 1527 when Bernardo Serena and his brother Filippo applied for a patent to make 'glass of stripes with twists of canes'. It is difficult to contemplate the incredible skill of glassmakers that could create such breathtaking designs. *Vetro à fili* used fine parallel or spiral stripes of white and other colours; *vetro à retorti* was made up of fine bands of intricate lacy patterns; and *vetro à reticello* captured a single air bubble in every criss-cross of fine white

A Venetian wine glass in vetro à reticello *with tiny trapped air bubbles within trellis, and a bottle in* vetro à retorti, *both from the 17th or early 18th century. Although small in scale, every piece is a* tour de force *of the glassmakers' skill.*

threads. These popular patterns continued to be made right up until the eighteenth century and precise dating is difficult, especially as identical glass was made elsewhere in Europe and Spain.

In spite of restrictions on their movement, glassmakers from Murano travelled in search of riches as far as Germany, Austria, Bohemia and England. In the sixteenth century it did not prove difficult to find financial backing to establish factories making glass *à la façon de Venise*. The best known centre of Venetian style glass was at Hall and nearby Innsbruck in the Austrian Tyrol, while in Vienna other workers supplied wealthy customers. Cologne revived its ancient glassmaking traditions, while in France copies of Venetian patterns were made at Orléans and at Nevers. Nevers became famous for its glass 'toys', figurines and animals made of coloured glass formed at the lamp by Jacques Raux and others. Subjects were often Biblical, or else were from the *Commedia dell'arte,* for the Nevers figures owed their origins to glass figurines made half a century earlier in Venice.

In the Low Countries, Antwerp was a major glassmaking centre, attracting many of the finest Venetian workmen. Elsewhere in the Netherlands a great deal of Venetian style glass was made, again also as a result of many

A detail from a painting by Georg Glegel (1563-1638) depicting a Façon de Venise *vase. The artist was based in Frankfurt and so it is likely the vase will be from the Low Countries, especially as it is shown next to a Dutch Roemer. Still life paintings provide a valuable source of information on the origin and trade in Venetian style glass.*

Venetian glassmakers re-introduced rich colours previously used in Roman times. The surface of this cobalt blue flask is decorated with diamond point engraving. Mid-17th century. 6¼in. (16cm).

wealthy local patrons. However, apart from certain local specialities such as bell-shaped stirrup cups and drinking horns, today very little *façon de Venise* is attributed to Holland. Enamelled decoration, principally coats of arms and gilded borders, was added to filigree glass in Austria and Germany, and much diamond

point engraving was carried out in the Tyrol.

In northern Spain glassmaking was centred in Barcelona where, early in the sixteenth century, fine coloured goblets were made for Queen Isabella. Enamelled glass was made, heavily influenced by Islamic traditions, and although somewhat crude, the Spanish figure painting is rather fun. Various *latticino* patterns were made and blue trailing was applied to serpent stem glasses. Although these were not as fine or clear in colour as the best Venetian glass, specimens found a keen local Spanish market, especially the distinctive spouted wine vessels known as *porrón* and *cantaro*.

In England, Italian glassblowers first arrived from Antwerp in the mid-sixteenth century but stayed for only two years. Jean Carré, also from Antwerp, was granted a patent in 1567 to make window glass in London and he also made *façon de Venise.* Before his death in 1572, another Italian from Antwerp, Giacomo Verzelini, joined Carré. The patent granted to Verzelini in 1574 permitted him to make glass in London in the Venetian manner, and more importantly, the importation of any Venetian glass from abroad was strictly forbidden. This early English glass by Verzelini is today masquerading as *façon de Venise,* and cannot be identified with the exception of around a dozen goblets which were decorated in diamond point with English inscriptions,

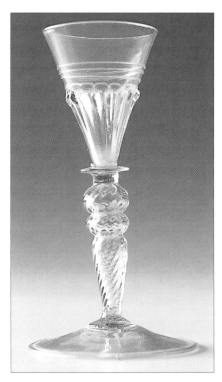

Venetian styles were copied with varying skill in different regions. This wine glass from Spain dates from the second half of the 17th century and is still well formed, although many designs became debased. 5⅜in. (13.5cm). Sandon collection

A bucket or 'aspersory' in Venetian 'Ice Glass' or cracquelé, *a clever use of material in an object possibly intended to contain real ice. Early 17th century. 6⅞in. (17.5cm) wide.*

added in London by a Frenchman, Anthony de Lysle. Verzelini retired in 1592 in favour of his sons who, along with others, continued to make glass in England

Throughout Europe in the sixteenth and early seventeenth centuries, much of the locally-made Venetian style glass was sold as if it were the real thing and had been imported from Venice. As kings and princes formed valuable collections, they cared little about the true origin. When Frederick IV of Denmark visited Italy in 1709 he was presented with several hundred pieces of Venetian glass to add to his vast collection. On the way home he

When the Duke of Newcastle visited Venice in 1741 with Horace Walpole he purchased a set of lattimo *plates painted in the Miotti workshop with views of Venice carefully copied from contemporary prints using a striking orange enamel. Horace Walpole purchased a similar set and, back in England, the plates were displayed as art treasures in Walpole's fantastic home, Strawberry Hill. 8¾in. (22.2cm) diameter.*

visited the King of Prussia to admire the new 'porcelain room' at Charlottenburg. Suitably impressed, the Danish king ordered a Glass Room to be built in his Rosenborg Palace to display his glass in a similar fashion. Construction was completed in 1714 and visitors to Copenhagen can still marvel at Frederick IV's collection of around 1,000 pieces of Venetian and *façon de Venise* glass, displayed in front of mirrors on gilded shelves. The collection has remained intact and contains specimens from most European glass factories including Austria, Germany and Scandinavia. The precise origin of each piece at Rosenborg sadly is not recorded. As a result ascribing glasses to any specific country is today seldom possible. Only in a few rare cases is any kind of definitive attribution possible, and so it is appropriate that the term *façon de Venise* is used more widely than 'Venetian'.

Much of the Venetian collection given to Frederick in 1709 was old stock from glass merchants, which was no longer saleable. Venetian glass had lost favour as engraved and cut glass from Bohemia became fashionable in the later seventeenth and eighteenth centuries. Traditional patterned glass from Murano enjoyed a revival in the nineteenth century, however. As collectors paid huge prices for old Venetian glass, a ready market grew for reproductions of enamelled bowls, serpent stemmed goblets and *latticino*. Just as Roman techniques had been reinvented during the Renaissance, late nineteenth century makers discovered how to make many of the intricate old Venetian patterns using glass recipes that had changed little since the sixteenth century. Little wonder that clever Victorian copies of old Venetian glass have been known to fool many experienced specialists.

Further reading

Rosa Barovier-Mentasti, *Il Vetro Veneziano*, Milan 1982

Hugh Tait, *The Golden Age of Venetian Glass*, British Museum Catalogue, London 1979

Hugh Tait (Ed.), *Five Thousand Years of Glass*, London 1991

Venetian vetro à retorti *glass with a rim of aventurine. This small bowl was made in the late 19th century using techniques unchanged for three hundred years, 2½in. (6.4cm) diameter.*

The Glass Room at the Rosenborg Palace in Copenhagen, completed in 1714. Frederick IV's vast collection included many pieces acquired on his visit to Venice in 1709.

CHAPTER 5

A Diffusion of Ideas

While Venice dominated the market in luxury glass for the great households throughout Europe, glass of a rather different kind was made for more general use. In total contrast to the clear *cristallo* of Venice, *Waldglas* or 'Forest Glass' originated in Germany and Northern Europe and followed quite separate traditions. Instead of using soda as a flux, glassmakers in Northern Europe used potash as the alkali in a different sort of glass distinguished by its impure green colouring, partly caused by a high iron content in the sand from which it was made. Forest glass was quite literally a product of the woodlands and forests which were systematically cleared to provide the great quantities of wood needed to fire the furnaces. Ash from the burnt wood used in the glass furnaces themselves provided the workers with potash, in particular wood from beech trees, supplemented by the product of

burning ferns and bracken which are a naturally rich source of the necessary alkali. Mobile glassmaking workshops moved from place to place, often into uninhabited mountain regions until the supply of wood was exhausted. Extensive deposits of sand and appropriate wood for fuel were available in Lorraine, Thuringia, Hessen, Bohemia and Southern England. Forest glass mostly sold locally, although significant trade routes developed supplying drinking glasses for taverns and ordinary households across all of Europe.

Manufacturing methods were strictly controlled, as they had been in Venice. In Germany powerful Guilds insisted glassworks remained only in families who could pass their secrets on through succeeding generations. Progress was naturally slow and traditional shapes of drinking vessels were made more or less unchanged for centuries. Shapes were

Left: a Krautstrunk *or 'cabbage stalk' tumbler, and right: a* Maigelein *beaker, simple examples of the 'Forest Glass' used domestically in the Netherlands, Germany and France. Few survive intact and consequently examples are expensive. Krautstrunk end 15th century, 6in. (15cm).*   Sotheby's/Kiddell papers

A Berkemeyer, *the forerunner of the* Roemer. *The applied prunts allow a firm grip to the stem of this popular drinking glass from the 15th or early 16th century. About 4¾in. (12cm) high.*   Sotheby's/Kiddell papers

Waldglas was used for all kinds of medical utensils and apparatus, as well as phials for dispensing medicine. These examples, excavated in England, date from the 17th century. With typical iridescence caused by burial, such phials are frequently mistaken for Roman glass. Largest 5¾in. (14.5cm).
Sandon collection

essentially functional rather than decorative. Their forms can often be traced back to the Frankish and Teutonic glass of the Dark Ages. Beakers were now given feet on which to stand, and the claw ornaments of the sixth to eight centuries developed into prunts which decorated stems of tumblers or *Berkemeyers*. These were more than ornamental, however, for prunted stems allowed a firm grip in a drunken hand. *Berkemeyers* were produced from the eleventh century and were often of large size, for German drinkers consumed large quantities of wine and beer. In time, Forest glassworks were able to make reasonably clear glass for windows, but the impure pale green colour had become popular with drinkers and for drinking vessels the makers emphasised this by adding copper oxide to the mix. Plain low bowl-like cups called *Maigeleins* were popular in France and the Netherlands in the fifteenth century, while in the Rhineland these were replaced in the mid-fifteenth century by a new shape of glass

called *Krautstrunk* or 'cabbage stalk', narrow ovoid shapes with large applied prunts. Most were used and broken during drunken festivities, but some of these most secular objects have, curiously, survived in perfect condition in cathedral treasuries where they were used as reliquaries to contain the precious bones of saints.

Cabbage stalk beakers were replaced in the sixteenth century by the forerunners of the *Roemers* which gradually dominated Northern European drinking habits. Prunts were restricted to the stems and the bowls were left plain now that the green glass could be made with fewer imperfections. A version of Venetian *cristallo* was made in Germany and the Netherlands using Forest glass purified by added manganese, but the use of this was limited initially to special presentation glasses which were enamelled or engraved for important occasions. Such pieces included *Stagenglasser,* a type of tall cylindrical glass with a domed lid, their form quite intentionally

A detail from a still life by Jeremias van Winghen, a painter active in Frankfurt c.1607. Rhenish wine is served in the new-style pale green Roemer, *while a delicate* façon de Venise *goblet is used for red wine. This probably came from glassworks at Innsbruck or from the Netherlands.*

phallic for these were popular marriage gifts.

During the seventeenth century some green glass *Roemers* were made of very large size to allow a host to show off his prowess at downing the contents in one draught. For a similar purpose cylindrical glass *Humpen* could hold a quart or two of beer. Many other shapes of German glass reflected local drinking habits. The *Pasglas* was a slender vessel marked with horizontal bands down its length. As the name implies, these were passed around a group of drinkers who in turn would take a drink and skilfully stop at the next line. If too much or too little was drunk and the line was missed, the drinker would face a forfeit which probably meant downing the rest of the *Pasglas* and re-filling it for his friends to continue their round. Another popular shape was the *Kuttrolf,* a kind of bottle with a neck formed from a number of spiralling tubes. These slowed the passage of liquid from the bottle so that a drink could be sipped or slowly savoured drop by drop.

Waldglas was certainly not restricted to Germany or the Low Countries. In England from around 1300 glassmakers were established in the Weald, in Surrey and Sussex, and by the sixteenth century Forest glass was made in many parts of England, France and Scandinavia. Drinking glasses were very much a sideline in most cases, for the principal product of most glassworks was window-panes. Also, as alchemy was practised throughout Europe, glassblowers were asked to make all manner of phials for dispensing perfumes and ointments, retorts for experimental apparatus, urine bottles and above all hourglasses. In provincial Spain a very distinctive and indeed rustic type of Forest glass was made in Almeria and Andalusia, including vases with pincered and nipped handles and irregular trailing. Some glass of a Forest type was even made in Italy, although this was totally overshadowed by the products of Venice.

Ironically, while we know *Waldglas* was made in enormous quantities, it is today amongst the rarest glass in the world. Most of it was purely functional and it was simply used until it got broken. Our knowledge of most of the shapes are the result of archaeology and while it is possible to buy examples which have been dug up and reconstructed, even a badly damaged *Krautstrunk* or *Berkemeyer* will cost you £1,000 or more. Roman glass is much older, but also much cheaper and far more plentiful. Ancient glass survives because intact objects were placed in graves, but from the Middle Ages this did not happen.

While Forest glass was essentially for everyday use and was left plain, German glassmakers from the sixteenth century used enamelling to create rather more important objects. Many inscribed and dated presentation pieces were produced for display as well as for ceremonial drinking, and their decoration reflected this. *Humpen* were the most splendid of all German glass shapes, for their large size and plain surface made them ideal canvases for glass enamellers. Bright colours, derived initially from Venice, were thickly applied and heightened with careful details which were picked out in black. Jewelled borders were filled with gold leaf in the Venetian tradition. These magnificent *Humpen,* some holding two quarts, were intended to make a political point as their owners would drink a toast to the Holy Roman Empire and its complicated constitution. The Imperial Eagle beakers or *Reichsadlerhumpen* were made virtually unchanged from at least 1571 until the end of the seventeenth century. These were painted with the most splendid double eagle, its wings emblazoned with a formal representation of the political structure of the Empire and its Electors – the princes who appointed the Emperor. The seven Electors also appear in all their glory on *Churfurstenhumpen,* dressed in their finest regalia or seated on comical horses. There is a charming cartoon quality to much of the painting on German *Humpen,* a kind of folk painting which sadly was not difficult to

A magnificent German Churfurstenhumpen *depicting the seven rulers of the Holy Roman Empire. The Emperor and each Elector is shown proudly on horseback, in a kind of naïve folk painting that has all the fun of a cartoon. This example is dated 1620. 13in. (33cm).*

forge. Many superb fakes of colourful *Humpen* were made in the nineteenth century and entered the best collections at the time. Today experts find this a most controversial area of study.

Other rather more simple examples of

A German enamelled flask for schnapps or a similar strong liqueur, sealed with a pewter screw top. Such flasks were enormously popular in the 18th century and offer much scope for collectors. 6½in. (16. 5cm).

enamelled. Vast quantities were made, usually painted in charming folk style with comical figures, formal flowers or drinking toasts written in archaic script. Eighteenth century examples are readily available to collectors today and although copies abound, it is not difficult to learn to tell these apart.

A change in the use of decoration on glass occurred in the Netherlands in the seventeenth century. The popularity of fine plain shapes such as *Roemers* and bottles was combined with the availability of diamonds and a new hobby was cultivated. In Tudor days lovesick poets began to write on window-panes and this led in due course to the fashion for calligraphy drawn on glassware with a diamond point. A hundred years after Anthony de Lysle inscribed names on Verzelini's London glass, an amateur decorator achieved notoriety in Holland for her

By the mid-17th century, the Roemer *has become a standard shape with 'raspberry prunts' applied to the hollow stem. This Dutch example is decorated with diamond point calligraphy in the style of Willem Jacobsz van Heemskerk.* Sotheby's/Kiddell papers

German enamelling have also attracted the attention of the forger. Several distinctive shapes of spirit flasks were made from the early seventeenth century, usually fitted with pewter mounts holding screw stoppers. Early examples were normally in coloured glass blown into moulds. From the end of the seventeenth century the usual shape was rectangular with canted corners and these were made mostly in clear glass which was then flowing inscriptions. Anna Roemers Vischer used both diamond point and wheel engraving early in the seventeenth century to decorate the plain bowls of green *Roemers*. Her sister also did calligraphy and both occasionally engraved flowers. Their work inspired followers, one of whom became the greatest exponent of this particular craft. Willem Jacobsz van Heemskerk worked in the town of Leiden where he added the most intricate calligraphic script to plain coloured glass bottles and a lesser number of goblets. In van Heemskerk's work the artistic flourish was far more significant than the words of his text. His decoration was in total harmony with the plain shapes he engraved.

In progressive decades, a number of skilful amateurs used diamond point engraving, culminating in the work of two new masters in the eighteenth century who used the technique of stippling. In Dordrecht, Frans Greenwood copied well-known prints on to the bowls of wineglasses with enormous subtlety. His signed work is known from the 1720s until his death in 1761. Later in the century David Wolff used the stipple process with even greater delicacy, and it is not unknown for his work to slip through salerooms totally unnoticed, as unless held in just the right light, his cupids and portraits are almost impossible to see.

Returning to the seventeenth century, changes were occurring in the formula of European glass which was to have far greater impact on decoration. Bohemian glassworkers discovered potash combined with chalk created a clear colourless glass that was far more stable than the Italian *cristallo* had been, and consequently it could be cut with a wheel. Earlier, in Prague, King Rudolf II had engaged Casper Lehmann as his principal engraver of hardstone gems. From the end of the sixteenth century, Lehmann turned his skills to the cutting of glass plaques using fine polishing wheels to engrave portraits and exciting borders. Shortly before his death in 1622 Lehmann took on a gifted young pupil, Georg Schwanhardt, who soon proved himself to be an able successor. Schwanhardt moved to Nuremberg where the local glassmakers provided him with dramatic goblets in

wonderful, thin clear glass on multi-knopped lightweight stems. These were perfectly suited to the new type of delicate engraving. Georg Schwanhardt established a school of glass engraving where his two sons and other members of his family joined him, as well as the equally talented Johann Wolfgang Schmidt. Nuremberg glass of the later seventeenth century is outstanding.

With the new stable Bohemian glass, it was possible to create thicker goblets, and with this new development closer copies of treasured rock crystal could be made. At Hermsdorf in Silesia in the 1690s, Friedrich Winter and his brother Martin were masters of two new kinds of glass cutting. *Tiefschnitt* used deep intaglio cutting to resemble the best engraved crystal, while *Hochschnitt* carved designs in incredibly

The Venetian style cristallo *glass made in the Netherlands was popular with many skilled Dutch diamond-point engravers. This late 17th century flask is probably the work of Willem Mooleyser. 9¼in. (21cm).*

The best Dutch engravers favoured English lead glass in the 18th century. This faceted stem wine glass by David Wolff commemorates the creation of the Batavian Republic in 1795. 5⅛in. (13.2cm). Wolff was the finest exponent of the stipple engraving technique.

A fine Nuremberg goblet probably engraved by Heinrich Schwanhardt who learned glass engraving from his father. The complicated stem formed from a series of hollow knops is typical of Nuremberg.Third quarter 17th century. 10¼in. (26cm).

high relief using the wheel to cut away some of the background. These cutting methods were adopted at Potsdam and Warmbrun where patronage from the King of Prussia encouraged the manufacture of portrait goblets heightened with pure gold which shone through the brilliant glass.

This was a period of great experimentation, linked also to alchemy. In the search for the 'Philosopher's Stone' which it was believed would turn base metal into gold, many chemists examined the properties of gold. Johann Kunckel used gold chloride to make *Rubinglas,* a wonderful rich red colour which

looked sumptuous when mounted in real gold. More precious than gold at the time, Frederick IV placed some of Kunckel's gold ruby glass in his Glass Room at Rosenborg (see page 67), while other pieces were proudly owned by

Dutch glassmakers combined strong shapes with brilliant colours. This decanter is decorated with typical wide ribs and bears metal mounts engraved with an armorial. Late 17th century. 9⅞in. (25cm).

rival royal collections in Prussia and Saxony. Augustus in Saxony was desperate to make his own porcelain, and Kunckel along with other glass chemists experimented with *Milchglas*, the German equivalent of Venetian *lattimo* or milk glass. Some was enamelled to resemble porcelain, but generally this was not a prosperous venture.

Far more successful was the use of gold between layers of glass, the so-called *Zwichengoldglas* which revived the Roman technique of gold sandwich glass. Now, however, two layers of glass were carefully polished to fit perfectly within one another. Fine gold leaf was used to apply delicate pictures between the two vessels which were then sealed together. *Zwichengoldglas* was popular in Bohemia from the 1730s to the 1750s, but beware, for this is another of the valuable commodities which were much copied in the nineteenth century.

While the painting on *Humpen* and spirit flasks was generally crude, a far superior type of enamelling developed in the middle of the seventeenth century. The glassworks that supplied blank goblets to the Nuremberg engravers also provided blanks to independent enamellers who became known as *Hausmalerei*. Painting was popular in two monochrome

Two Bohemian Zwischengoldglas *tumblers. It took a great deal of skill to form two layers of glass that would fit closely together and protect the delicate gold and silver foil sandwiched between. c.1740. 3½in. (9cm).*

A German flask by Ignaz Preissler, an enameller from Breslau who specialised in Schwarzlot *decoration in black monochrome. Preissler's painting complements the elaborate Silesian glass cutting. c.1730-40. 6⅛in. (15.5cm).*

A Silesian goblet with characteristic moulded stem, displaying superb engraved decoration. The portrait of the Austro-Hungarian Emperor Franz 1 and armorial designs have been wheel engraved with particular care. c.1740. 9in. (23cm). The foot is a replacement made of silver.

colours, black – known as *Schwarzlot* – and iron red or *Eisenrot*. Occasionally these two colours were combined together and also very occasionally gold was added to pick out details in the *Schwarzlot*. The first master of this

transparent monochrome painting was Johann Schaper who painted delicate landscapes as well as spirited figure subjects and armorials on knopped-stem goblets and on distinctive low beakers with ball feet. Schaper was

Detail of a painting dated 1734 by Anton Friedrich Harms showing a Dutch wineglass with diamond-point decoration. The faceted cruet bottle is imported from Silesia. Flamboyant still life paintings serve to remind us that most treasured glass items were originally intended for everyday use.

followed at the end of the seventeenth century by Ignaz Preissler who worked at Breslau. Preissler is famous for his *Hausmaler* painting on Chinese and Meissen porcelain, especially in the Chinoiserie taste, a style he also mastered on Silesian glass.

Porcelain offered a far greater attraction to enamellers and very little painted glass of

consequence was produced in the eighteenth century. Fine wheel engraving continued to flourish, particularly in Bohemia and in Silesia. This was the age of the engraved presentation goblet, some of which are simply breathtaking. The shapes were either complicated copies of rock crystal, or else they had very plain bowls in generous proportions to show off the engraver's

A Prussian Royal commemorative covered goblet engraved with a portrait of Frederick William I and Sophie Dorothea of Prussia. The technique of filling the engraving with bright gold was a speciality of Potsdam and Berlin. c.1735-40. 12in. (30.5cm).

skill. These triumphant pieces, complete with tall covers, were treasured in families and consequently quite a lot survive. As a result they can seem reasonably priced today in view of the workmanship they represent.

In contrast to these goblets, many plain bucket-shaped tumblers were made in Bohemia and in Scandinavia, thick with deep but primitive cutting. Other plain engraved glass was made in Spain at La Granja de San Illdefonso, at an important glassworks established in 1728 north-west of Madrid. La Granja glass was lightweight and generally impure, and its floral engraving is often filled in with gold.

The best engravers in Continental Europe worked in Holland but were disappointed with the quality of local glassmaking. They preferred instead to use fine English lead glass which was imported without decoration. Glassmakers in Antwerp and Liège early in the eighteenth century produced glass *à la façon d'Angleterre,* and other English style glass was made in Holland, in Spain and in Norway. The confusion that results is discussed in the following chapter.

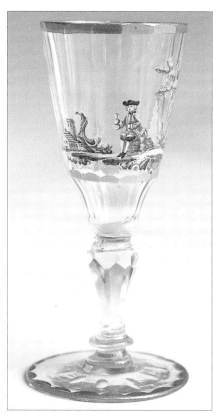

Bohemian enamelled decoration in the rococo taste is well suited to the finely fluted shape of this small wine glass. c.1770. 5⅜in. (13.5cm).

Venus chastising Cupid, engraved with a primitive charm on a typical thick German tumbler. c.1700. 4½in. (11.5cm). 18th century clear glass tumblers are fairly plentiful today and generally inexpensive.

Further reading

Olga Drahotvà, *European Glass,* London and New York 1983

Brigitte Klesse and Hans Mayr, *European Glass from 1500-1800, the Ernesto Wolf collection,* Vienna 1987

S. Petrova and J-L. Olivié, *Bohemian Glass,* Paris 1990

Ada Polak, *Glass, Its Makers and Its Public,* London 1975

A.G.A. van Dongen and H.E. Henkes, *Utility Glass in Image and Imagination,* Museum Boymans-van Beuningen, Rotterdam, 1994

CHAPTER 6

English Drinking Glasses

For more than a century before the Restoration, England had a productive glass industry, but only a few dozen examples can be identified. The reason is simple – Verzelini in the sixteenth century, and his successor Sir Robert Mansell in the seventeenth, engaged Venetian and Dutch glassworkers and made *cristallo* glass in the manner of the Venetians. It was not until the second half of the seventeenth century that a recognisable English vernacular style developed. Mansell was granted a patent in 1615 and, like Verzelini, he held the monopoly on English glassmaking. Up until this date glassmakers had used wood to fire their furnaces, but there was now an acute shortage of timber. Wood was needed instead to build ships and new

An English wine bottle of typical 'onion' shape in very basic, dark coloured glass. Early wine bottles are full of character and when plain (without seals) examples can be found at reasonable prices, c.1700. 7in. (18cm) high.

laws forced the glass industry to switch to coal-burning furnaces. Coal burned at higher temperatures, but the resulting coal fumes created many new problems that greatly hampered the progress of British glassmaking.

After Mansell's death in 1656, the valuable patents passed to the Duke of Buckingham who ran several different glassworks employing separate managers. A Frenchman, John de la Cam, ran the Duke's glassworks at Greenwich, while Thomas Tilson, Thomas Plowden and Martin Clifford supervised other ventures. All no doubt continued to employ Italian craftsmen and our failure to identify the mirrors and *façon de Venise* made in Greenwich and Vauxhall is also due to the continual importation of far superior *cristallo* glass from abroad. While England was politically divided during the Civil War, individual artistic and scientific endeavours were suppressed, and the glass industry continued to struggle with the use of coal.

Wine bottles, for filling from the cask, had traditionally been made of Rhenish stoneware. Following the Restoration in 1660, English-made glass bottles appeared and soon captured a valuable market. Utilitarian and robust, these were made for taverns or wine merchants, or for aristocrats to use on their estates. To prevent pilfering, the ownership of many glass bottles was established by embossed initials, crests and dates which were stamped using seals on to applied blobs of glass on the shoulders of the bottles. The dated seals allow us to work out an exact chronology for the different shapes of English wine bottles. These begin in the 1660s with 'globe and shaft' types with round bodies below slender necks. These were followed by 'onion' shaped bottles popular from about 1690, characterised by high 'kick-in' bases which allowed the wine to cool quickly when the bottle was placed in ice. During the eighteenth century it is possible to follow the development of the modern cylindrical wine bottle. Early English wine bottles are the successors of Forest glass – dark, green and indelicate but totally functional. English bottles were widely exported to wine-producing countries. Today examples are sufficiently plentiful to have created a widespread collectors' market. Plain bottles start at less than £100 ($160), while particularly early shapes or dated sealed bottles can run to many thousands. Curiously, collectors regard 'iridescence' – a common deterioration of the surface resulting from burial in the ground – as an advantage and, as with Roman glass, rainbow iridescence adds appreciably to a bottle's value.

The wealthiest homes served wine in bottles made of beautifully clear lead glass that reflected the colour of their contents through the surface like a lens. The invention of lead glass revolutionised English glassmaking, for here was a product that could not only rival the Venetians, but in terms of clarity was far superior. The credit goes to George Ravenscroft who had been employed by the Glass Sellers' Company to research the nature of glass. Antonio Neri's 1612 book *Art of Glass* had just been translated into English and this undoubtedly helped Ravenscroft, who was also assisted by another Italian named da Costa. The first successful English 'Christaline Glasse' was produced around 1673 at Ravenscroft's Savoy glassworks on the Thames by the Strand and was the subject of a most valuable patent. The Glass Sellers' Company gave Ravenscroft financial backing enabling him to move in 1674 to a new glassworks at Henley-on-Thames. His new type of glass was made principally from flint with lead oxide as the flux, and was used to make wineglasses, jugs and serving bottles.

After 1677 Ravenscroft was sufficiently proud of his glass to mark some of his products with an applied seal of a raven's head. Ravenscroft's lead glass was far from perfect, for it was still prone to 'crizzling', the fault he had been determined to overcome. If the mix

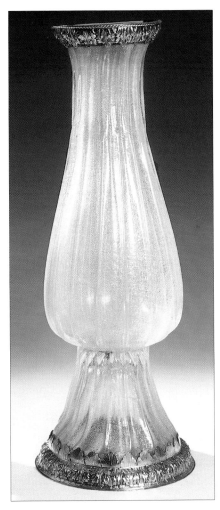

An early lead glass vase from the time of George Ravenscroft, fitted with important silver-gilt mounts. Ravenscroft's formula was prone to 'crizzling' — tiny internal cracks that give the glass a cloudy appearance. Very little lead glass from this period has survived, c.1675. 17in. (43cm).

was not quite right, as the glass cooled a network of tiny cracks could develop, or else these appeared over a period of years as the glass was used. The curious ice-like cloudiness

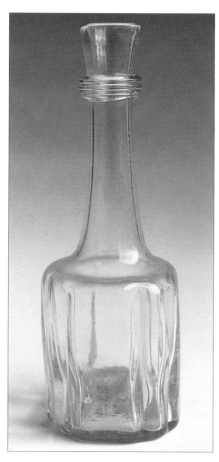

A 'Cruciform' decanter or serving bottle from the early 18th century. Made thickly from heavy lead glass, the shape was designed to assist the cooling of the wine when placed in ice. The rim is not ground inside, for early decanters did not have stoppers, c.1710-20. 10⅝in. (27cm).

soon replaced by well-washed sand, but the name 'flint glass' continued to be used to describe English lead glass, leading to much confusion later. Lead glass versions of continental shapes such as *Roemers* and plain bottles can have a foreign feel, while other very English shapes such as posset pots were made, their shapes inspired by English delftware.

Mostly, however, the forms of English glass were derived from metal prototypes in silver or pewter. Ceremonial goblets and covered cups were decorated with moulded flutes and hollow knopped stems copying metalwork. Parallels with pewter provide a guide to dating, but a precise chronology is far from easy. Coins placed within the hollow stems of glasses ought to assist, but these are notoriously unreliable, as glassworkers seem frequently to have used older coins.

The use of lead oxide became widespread and within only a few years the problems Ravenscroft had experienced with crizzling were almost totally eradicated. English glass was brilliantly clear and, when struck, was resonant like a bell. The high clarity, and freedom from impurities allowed light to refract through a glass, apparently transmitting a mystic glow from within. This English 'glass of lead' called for robust shapes, as the melted glass mix was not as tactile as *façon de Venise*. Wafer thin bowls and trailed serpent stem ornament became both impractical and unfashionable, replaced with rather bolder flutes, solid knops and coarse trailed and pincered decoration. A Venetian pattern of criss-cross ornament became popular, formed on the bowls of wineglasses and bases of bottles or decanters. A contemporary reference used by Ravenscroft in 1675 gave this pattern a name of 'nipt diamond waies', a much-misused term some collectors like to apply to glass made several centuries after Ravenscroft's time.

The study of English drinking glasses relies on a very precise classification of stem and bowl types. This methodical classification was formulated by collectors at the beginning of the twentieth century and has gradually evolved, thanks mostly to the published work of Barrington Haynes in the 1950s and L.M.

known as crizzling can occur in other Continental soda glass and does not always indicate an early date

Unmarked pieces are hard to ascribe, for several new glasshouses began to make flint glass, not only in England but in the Netherlands too, all using lead oxide as the flux. In the interest of greater purity, flint was

A selection of fine 'Heavy Baluster' wine glasses. From left: a bell bowl on a double drop knop stem and a domed foot; a teared funnel bowl above a three-ring annulated knop and a teared inverted baluster knop; a plain funnel bowl on an angular knop and teared basal knop: right: a rounded funnel bowl and rare egg knop containing a tear. All have folded feet, the largest 9 in. (23cm).

Bickerton in the '60s. Bickerton's detailed classification is still widely accepted and used by most specialists today. There are, of course many variables, but the principal groups begin around 1700 with the 'heavy balusters', followed by 'balustroids' or 'light balusters' from the 1720s. Named after a supporting feature seen in architecture and furniture, balusters are classified according to the shape and number of knops from which the stems are formed. A knop is basically a decorative shape in the stem and can range from a simple swelling to a complicated group of rings in different sizes. The names are purely descriptive – ball, cushion, acorn, mushroom and so on, and sometimes these can be the right way up (true) or upside down (inverted). Knops can be hollow, teared (containing a single tear shaped bubble) or beaded (with tiny beads of air trapped inside the knop). Amongst the rarest and most sought after knops are egg or cylinder shapes. Some makers were more

skilful than others, and collectors look for a good balance and even proportions, as well as glass of high clarity. With few faults within the glass, English wine glasses did not need to hide behind cutting or engraving which could disguise defects – the reason Continental glass was frequently faceted.

Distinctive shaped stems, believed to have originated in Silesia, were copied in England using moulds to produce hexagonal or octagonal baluster knops. These English stems became known as 'Silesian stems' (although nowadays the term 'pedestal stem' is more generally used). Extra details moulded on to pedestal stems include stars, crowns or 'God Save King George', referring to the coronation in 1715. Later in the eighteenth century debased forms of pedestal stems were frequently used to support tazzas.

Bowls and feet have their own classifications. During the baluster period bowls were mostly plain, slightly curving funnel shapes.

A collection of sweetmeat (or champagne) glasses from 1720-40. Most have double ogee bowls with or without honeycomb moulding. The stems are either pedestals (or Silesian stems) or else balusters including a rare acorn knop and a bobbin knop. The example on the right is wheel-cut with facets and dates from about forty years later than the others.

There is much discussion as to the intended use of glasses with rather wide open bowls which are often moulded with flutes or panels. These are normally placed on pedestal stems and are known either as sweetmeat glasses or as champagne glasses. Both terms are probably correct, for the fashion for drinking champagne from shallow, open glasses probably developed out of glasses used for serving jellies or sweetmeats.

The feet of early wineglasses were conical so that the 'pontil', the rough scar in the centre of the base, would be raised up inside and would not scratch a precious polished table. Many baluster glasses have 'domed' feet that raise the centre up more gracefully. Feet were generally wide to give stability. To prevent chipping, the edges of feet were frequently reinforced by folding the rim back on itself and flattening the edge underneath. Delicate 'folded feet' had been occasionally used by the Venetians, but the English glassmakers produced robust versions that gave their glass great strength. It is very unusual to find folded feet that have chipped.

Baluster stemmed wine glasses are very expensive and mostly beyond the reach of novice collectors. Any decent baluster glass will be over £1,000 ($1,600) and rarities are very costly. Curiously, however, sweetmeat or champagne glasses of the same period are much more reasonable and I think offer scope for a beginner, for they can be found for as little as £200-£400 ($320-$650).

The heavy balusters are aptly named, for solid knops of lead glass add much weight to the chunky glasses. The threat of tax on glass determined by weight brought about change. Light balusters, or 'balustroids', are not simply thinner and lighter versions of baluster glasses. During this next phase of English drinking glass production, stems were made much more thinly, but with simplification came far less flare and excitement. A series of small knops does not have the magic of a big bold stem, but towards the middle of the eighteenth century the mood in England was for simple elegance, not heavy baroque grandeur. Picture the scene at the Kit Kat Club in London, immortalised by Kneller's portrait showing fashionably dressed gentlemen drinking from wineglasses with light baluster stems and gently elegant bowls.

Two superb 'Newcastle' wine goblets with wheel engraving added in Holland. One depicts an allegory of Friendship while the other bears the arms of the various Dutch provinces. The light baluster stems include typical beaded knops. c.1745-50. 7⅞in. (20cm).

These are the glasses you would take to your picnic in Ranelagh Gardens. Where larger knops are present they are hollow or filled with delicate patterns of twisted air bubbles.

Light balusters culminated around 1740 in a kind of superior version associated with Newcastle. There is plenty of evidence that these finest English wineglasses were made in the North-east, as Newcastle upon Tyne was a major production centre from where a thriving export trade took the best 'Newcastle balusters' to The Netherlands. The top engravers working in Holland bought Newcastle glasses because they were the best in Europe, combining strength with delicacy, elegant bowls with multiple knopped stems full of beads that sparkled. These were so popular in Holland that today it is hard to find a Newcastle glass without Dutch engraving. The value depends largely on the nature of the engraving rather than the stem.

There are plenty of affordable glasses available from the 1730s and '40s. I refer here to the 'plain stems', wineglasses with bowls known as 'drawn trumpets', extending from the foot to the rim of the bowl in a gentle unbroken curve. The stems are often lightened by a single large tear and the feet are often folded. Examples still rarely cost more than £100 ($160) and for this have all the character of English lead glass.

It has been claimed that the development of the 'air twist' stem was due entirely to the tax on glass, but there has to be more to it than that. The glassmaker's skill as he juggled the tiny bubbles into spiralling corkscrews suited entirely the spirit of rococo in the England of Handel and Chelsea porcelain. Air twists are often referred to as Mercurial stems, a great misnomer, for although the shimmering light inside the twist looks like the metallic shine of liquid mercury, it is all a trick of the light and the spiral bubbles contain nothing but air. The age of the air twist stem was from roughly 1745-1760, when it gave way to the 'opaque twist'. Also known as 'lace twist' or 'cotton twist' stems, these incorporate spiralling patterns of milk white glass instead of air bubbles. The technology owes much to the Venetians and their *latticino* glass but, now captured within clear English lead glass, the opaque twists have a precision the Venetians had never been able to achieve.

As with previous knopped stems, collectors work to a precise chronology for air twists and opaque twists. A plain corkscrew or spiral band on its own is known as a 'single series' twist. If encircled by further bands or spirals a stem becomes a 'double series'. When spiralling strands are too numerous to count they are often referred to as 'multiple spirals'. Component threads or ribbons are usually formed in multiples of two and so reference is made to a 'pair of spiral bands' or to 'two pairs of threads' rather than four. Assisted by a magnifying glass, it is possible to count the number of tiny threads making up a 'multi-ply' twist and in some double series opaque twist stems it is possible to find twelve-ply, fifteen-ply and even twenty-ply spiral bands, often perfectly formed.

Twist stem glasses can have additional knops that tend to distort the internal pattern. In the 1740s rare 'composite stem' glasses place lengths of air twist between separate plain and knopped sections. Collectors look out for these and other rare variations of drinking glass stems. 'Mixed twist' stems combine air and opaque twists together in a single pattern. 'Incised twist' stems feature fine spiralling grooves formed on the outside surface of the stem. The rarest of all are the 'colour twists' where tiny threads of blue, red, green or yellow are included in otherwise white opaque twist stems. All colours were difficult to control and are scarce, commanding high prices. 'Canary yellow' is the rarest of all, and a fine example can be worth in excess of £10,000 ($15,000). Colour twist stems were popular in Holland and many were made there in a coarse soda glass. Many novice collectors have rushed to show me an exciting 'find', a wine glass with bell-shaped bowl and red colour twist stem, worth maybe £3,000-£5,000 ($4,500-$7,500) if English, and I have to tell them gently that their glass is Dutch with a value only around £100 ($150).

Many English glasses were copied in Holland as well as in Norway in the eighteenth century. It is only in recent years that research has shown the extent of a thriving glass industry at Nostetangen in Norway making lead glass. A number of light baluster glasses formed of a dark coloured metal, once thought to be English without question, are now suspected to have been made in Norway. Excavations have also shown that lead glass continued to be made in Holland in the eighteenth century. The attribution of some potentially very valuable English glasses has become controversial, and this is an area where more research and an open mind is needed.

The high quality and consistency of English air twist and opaque twist stems has led to a largely stable market. Plain examples are still reasonably priced, but values have certainly risen in recent years. Value is determined mostly by the shape and decoration on the bowl. Drinking glass bowls were adapted for different kinds of drink. Wine was usually strong and fortified, and so bowls were always much smaller than the wineglasses of today. 'Rounded funnel' or 'ogee' shapes are the most commonly encountered, while bell, thistle or pan-topped shapes are always more expensive. Fruit cordials called for glasses with tiny bowls which were usually placed on very tall stems. Beer was mostly drunk from tankards, but a kind of strong ale, resembling present day barley wine, was served in elegant households in glasses with very tall, slender bowls. Engraved decoration can often indicate the intended use of a drinking glass. Ale glasses were engraved with a spray of hops and barley. Cordial glasses can depict berries or fruit, while very rare cider glasses are engraved with apples or apple trees.

Engraved decoration opens up a great big area of glass collecting. Simple borders were engraved on early baluster wineglasses, while Holland introduced the fashion for more decorative engraving on Newcastle glasses. Engravers in England during the 1740s-1760s used grinding wheels to cut all sorts of patterns on to wineglasses, especially flowers. Some flower sprays are purely decorative, while others had much deeper significance to their original owners who understood a special 'code'. Supporters of the Jacobite claim to the throne of England pledged their allegiance to the Stuart descendants of James I and in particular to Prince Charles Edward Stuart – known as Bonnie Prince Charlie. They could not proclaim their support openly, and so hid the subject of their affection in secret emblems that only fellow Jacobites could understand.

The large number of Jacobite glasses that survive suggests that the Jacobites were both numerous and unafraid, for the secret insignia is often rather prominent. Everywhere we find the Jacobite rose, a formal depiction of a wild

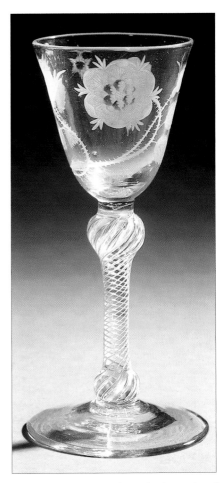

An air twist wine glass with 'Jacobite' engraving of a formal rose with two buds, an oak leaf and a star — emblems with hidden meanings to supporters of the cause. The stem is a multiple spiral air twist with shoulder and basal knop. c.1750. (15cm).

rose fully open with either one or two closed buds. Stars, oak leaves and Latin mottoes accompany Jacobite roses and the most valued of all – portraits of Bonnie Prince Charlie himself. The romantic story of the Jacobites appealed greatly to Victorian and early twentieth century collectors who paid serious

A series of six details of wine glass stems.

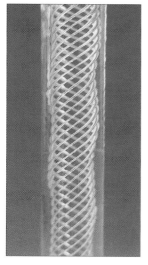

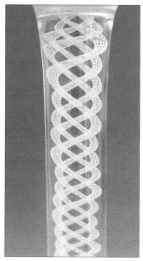

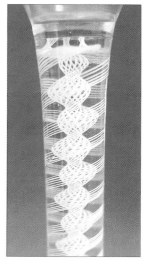

A multiple spiral air twist stem with a cable set in clear glass, c.1750.

A single series opaque twist stem with two pairs of spiral gauzes, c.1760.

A double series opaque twist stem with a multi-ply corkscrew within a pair of six-ply spiral bands, c.1765.

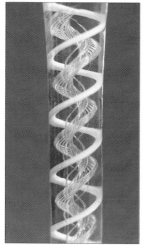

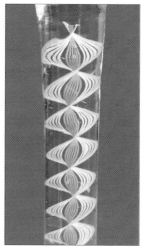

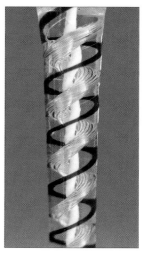

A mixed twist stem, with a multi-ply spiral air cable within a single opaque spiral thread, c.1765-70.

A colour twist stem with a multi-ply corkscrew stranded in white and canary yellow. A great rarity, c.1770.

A mixed colour twist stem, with a multi-ply air spiral, an opaque white heavy cable and a deep blue spiral thread, c.1765-70.

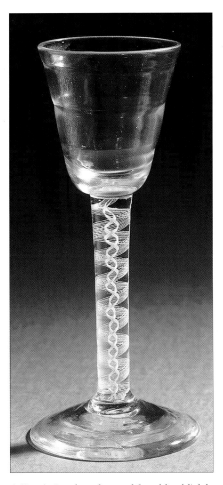

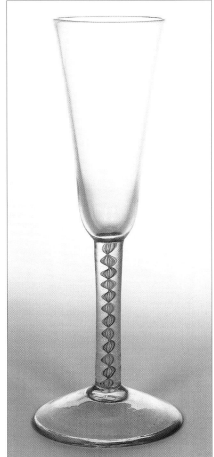

A 'Lynn' wine glass, the round funnel bowl lightly moulded with the horizontal bands associated with East Anglian glassmaking, on a double series opaque twist stem, c.1760-70.

A colour twist ale glass with the characteristic tall bowl used for drinking strong, fortified ale. This extremely rare stem combines threads of blue, yellow and white in a single corkscrew, c.1770. 7⅞in. (20cm).

prices for such glasses. Sadly there were insufficient genuine glasses to fill the demand, and fakes were created in quantity. Many Victorian and Edwardian copies are blatant, on glasses of quite absurd shape and size. However, a great many genuine but plain eighteenth century air twist and opaque twist glasses were

given fake engraving copying the precious Jacobite originals. (See also Chapter 1, page 33, on fakes).

The manufacture of porcelain in England in the mid-eighteenth century led to widespread use of enamelling on chinaware. Curiously, glass proved very difficult to enamel, or else it

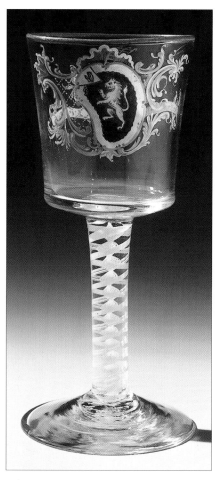

A fine armorial goblet enamelled by the Beilbys in Newcastle. The arms of the Gray family are painted within a flowing rococo cartouche, a hallmark of the Beilby workshop. With bucket bowl and double series opaque twist stem. c.1770. 7⅝in. (19.5cm.)

William Beilby and his sister Mary were retailers in Newcastle upon Tyne selling fine glassware, some of which they enamelled. In the 1760s rococo was still in fashion and the Beilbys mastered the subtlety of rococo ornament, painted on to the bowls of wineglasses using opaque white enamel. Delicate white vines suspended from gilded rims came to life when dark red wine filled the glass. Landscapes were subtle too, with cartoon figures and birds among ruins, fluffy trees and scrollwork. Decanters bore proud labels for exotic foreign wines within the most exuberant rococo cartouches. Beilby's crowning glory was armorial decoration, an idiom rarely used in England before. Commissions from English and Dutch royalty led to magnificent goblets, well deserving of their high value today.

Beilby is the only name linked to enamelling on British wineglasses. The discovery of a number of white painted glasses in Scotland, however, has led to a rethinking and it has to be presumed that Newcastle was not the only centre for enamelling. Painting of a different kind was practised in South Staffordshire using opaque white glass rather than clear. White glass vases and scent bottles were painted in colours with decoration closely related to contemporary porcelain and the enamelled metal trinkets that were produced also in Staffordshire around Birmingham and at nearby Bilston. Deep blue glass scent bottles match some of the enamelling on the opaque white pieces, and these must also have a Staffordshire origin.

Just as Beilby's name is used rather too freely, so too is that of James Giles, for all gilded decoration on English glass is usually attributed to just one workshop. At Giles' studio in Soho, London around 1770, fine gold foliage or vines were added to both clear and deep blue glass, and as neo-classical design became fashionable gilt rams' heads hung with husk garlands were gilded with great care. In the absence of signed specimens it is possible to find some links to Giles decoration on porcelain, but it is difficult to ascribe any piece with certainty. Gilding was not effective on clear drinking glasses and consequently

was simply unfashionable in the age of fine engraving. Whatever the reason, painted decoration is very rarely found on English glass and all examples are understandably expensive today.

The only name that seems to matter in English enamelled glass is that of Beilby.

Decoration in enamel or gold is rare on English glass and of much interest to collectors, greatly increasing the value of otherwise standard opaque twist stem wine glasses. Left: white enamel fruit and birds associated with the Beilby workshop in Newcastle. Right: gilded vines added in James Giles' workshop in London's Soho. Both c.1770. 5½in. (14.2cm).

examples are rare and expensive. It was not until the end of the eighteenth century, with the popularity of coloured glass, that gilding came into its own.

Fashion changed in the 1770s as rococo gave way to the classical taste. Opaque twist stems on glasses were replaced by facet cutting that matched the style of new cut glass

chandeliers. Clear glass stems cut with perfectly formed diamonds or hexagons sparkled in the light and supported thicker and larger bowls as drinking fashions changed also. The faceted stems became shorter and cut decoration extended into the base of the bowls in petal-like patterns. Clever cutting can sometimes reveal the shape of a rose or other

Three small glasses with handles intended for syllabub, together with a cup for posset with an applied spout. Glasses for jelly or syllabub without handles are reasonably plentiful, but handled examples are scarce. The 'double B' handles on the left are particularly rare, All first half of the 18th century. 4⅛in. and 3½in. (10.5cm. and 9cm).

A hexagonal faceted stem dates this wine glass to 1770-80 when political events attracted serious support. This glass, commissioned to endorse the cause of John Wilkes, is inscribed 'Liberty and Wilkes' above an engraved birdcage — an emblem of liberty. 5½in. (13.8cm).

A nest of tazzas or footed comports in graduated sizes, used as stands for cakes or jelly and custard glasses. With debased versions of the pedestal stem, tazzas enjoyed great popularity at the end of the 18th century.

'Dwarf ale' or 'short ale' glasses with conical bowls and short stems were used for strong beer or barley wine. These examples with 'wrythen' moulding date from the late 18th century and are very popular with collectors.

flower when you look down into the bowl of a wineglass. In the 1780s the French taste for simple engraved borders became fashionable in England, especially rings of formal plants or leaves, or repeated ovals and crosses which have become known as 'oxo' borders.

While the stems of wineglasses became short, ale glasses lost their stems altogether. New 'short ale' or 'dwarf ale' glasses were placed on very rudimentary stems or narrow 'bladed knops', while spiral moulding became popular on a class of small glasses known as 'wrythen ales'. Some short ales were still engraved with the distinctive hops and barley, but when left plain it is difficult to tell if the small conical glasses were used for strong ale or for jellies and syllabubs which were increasingly popular. These sweet confections were served in individual glasses placed on tiers of glass tazzas or on silver trays. Apart from expensive rarities such as glasses with double handles, or spouted posset glasses, these jellies are generally cheap. Many charming small ale or jelly glasses are available for the beginning collector, along with patty pans or tart pans that were used to serve individual pâtés or sweetmeats as side dishes on a table. Such simple objects (as illustrated on page 41) are ideal introductions to eighteenth century English glass for they rarely cost much at all.

Further reading

E. Barrington Haynes, *Glass Through the Ages,* London 1948

L.M. Bickerton, *Eighteenth Century English Drinking Glasses,* Woodbridge, 1986

Robert Charleston, *English Glass and the Glass Used in England,* London 1984

Geoffrey Seddon, *The Jacobites and their Drinking Glasses,* Woodbridge, 1997

James Rush, *A Beilby Odyssey,* Olney, 1987

CHAPTER 7

The Age of Cut Glass

The glass industry in Britain was continually threatened by taxation. In addition to the window tax, in 1745/46 new Glass Excise Acts had imposed taxes on the weight of different kinds of manufactured glass. The inevitable result was a demand for thinner and thus lighter shapes in table glass, as well as the movement of a large part of the industry to

The elegant shape of Georgian ship's decanters make them very popular today. While the wide bases helped to keep them stable on board ship, such decanters were also used ashore in grand houses. This example, with a bull's-eye stopper and four neck rings, dates from around 1800. 9¼in. (23.5cm).

Ireland in an attempt to avoid the taxes. There were various ways to try and avoid duty. At the Nailsea glassworks, established near Bristol by John Lucas at the end of the eighteenth century, luxury objects were made using cheap materials to avoid the duty on fine glass. Instead of costly clear glass, jugs and decanters were made from dark green bottle glass decorated with coloured splashes (illustrated on page 47). Similar products were made in other provincial centres such as Alloa in Scotland and at Wrockwardine in Shropshire, and attributions to specific glassworks are therefore impossible.

Bristol had become a major centre for glass manufacture. Although coloured glass had been made all over Britain, not least around Birmingham in the 1750s and '60s, the numerous glassmakers in Bristol seemed to specialise in the use of colour. As a result the name of Bristol is closely associated with deep blue glass in particular. The general acceptance of the Bristol origin is due in part to one Bristol maker, Isaac Jacobs, who signed a number of blue finger bowls and plates to which he added armorials and border designs in gilding. Aside from these, the frustrating lack of any marked pieces has led to much confusion. James Giles, the London enameller and gilder, is known to have bought glass from the Falcon glass house in Southwark (later managed by Apsley Pellatt) and much of Giles' gilding was on blue glass scent bottles and decanters. While it is unlikely that Giles bought his blue glass in Bristol, a lot of coloured glass probably was made in the Bristol area, and the name has become synonymous with all English coloured glass.

Green was the most popular colour for luxury wineglasses at the beginning of the nineteenth century. The simple conical shaped bowls were raised usually on a short stem with

94

A set of three club shaped decanters of Bristol type in deep green glass, gilded with labels for their original contents. These would have fitted into a silver or plated stand. The stoppers should always be gilded with the correct initial letter. Look out for examples that have been re-gilded at a later date. c.1810. 9in. (23cm).

a single bladed knop, and sets were supplied with similar coloured decanters, usually sold in threes. Amethyst was a difficult colour to control, but also proved popular. Pale blue, amber and even red were added to the repertoire early in the nineteenth century, but deep blue remained by far the most popular colour for decanters. Here there is a curious anomaly. While numerous green wineglasses were made, it is almost impossible to find sets of blue glasses from the period.

From about 1780 until 1815 or so, it was usual for the coloured glass decanters to be gilded with labels indicating their contents. Sets of three, inscribed 'Brandy', 'Rum' and

'Hollands' (a type of gin) sold in silver-plated or lacquered stands. Examples are not particularly rare today, but are much sought after, especially when the gilding of the labels remains fresh and has not worn at all. Make sure the stoppers match – they should always have corresponding initial letters in gold, R for Rum and so on. Some worn coloured decanters have been re-gilded at a much later date and can look simply too bright. Also watch out for tiny scratches on the surface of decanters that disappear underneath the gilding, a telltale sign that the gold has been replaced.

While Continental glassmakers were discovering colour to a much greater extent, in

An 18th century English or Irish table candelabrum formed from sections of cut glass cut with facets to reflect the candle light. c.1770.

candles was reflected and thus multiplied. Orders flooded in and earned fortunes for the best glasshouses capable of constructing the new classical styles of chandeliers. With the new taste, the English glasscutter could really show off his skill. Spires supported glass stars, moons and crescents alternating with nozzles hung with garlands of graduated pear-shaped beads. Faceted pendent drops would catch the light like a myriad of valuable diamonds – indeed fine candelabras and chandeliers were as costly as prized jewellery. Using metal frameworks, chandeliers could be constructed to massive proportions, with strings of sparkling beads cascading all around. By the height of the Regency period fine chandeliers could cost several thousand pounds and were designed to dazzle guests by their brilliance. Wall lights would match standing table candelabra, raised on bases of the best ormolu or set with bronze statues or encircled by bands of Wedgwood jasperware with classical reliefs.

Lead glass had been made in Ireland since the seventeenth century, and from about 1760 cutting was important here also. The Glass Excise Acts benefited Ireland greatly, for the most stringent regulations imposed in England did not apply in Ireland until much later. From the 1780s coal was not taxed when used in glass furnaces and Ireland could trade freely with England. Consequently many English glassmakers set up factories in Ireland, sending skilled workers to train local craftsmen. The glass industry flourished in Ireland, at least until 1825 when a new Glass Excise Act was applied there too, causing a sharp decline in the glassmakers' fortunes and the subsequent resurgence of Birmingham and Stourbridge.

It is far from easy to identify Irish glass. It is seldom appreciated that the composition of Irish glass is identical to English. The supposedly unique grey coloured metal beloved by collectors of old Irish glass is partly due to the imported sand, for at Waterford glass was made using sand specially shipped in from Kings Lynn in Norfolk. Also, in a further attempt to evade duty, it was not unknown for English makers to smuggle some of their glass into Ireland and pretend it had a local origin.

Britain coloured glass was relatively unimportant alongside the vast production of colourless cut glass. Cutting had been practised since the early eighteenth century but its use expanded greatly in the 1770s with the fashion for faceted stems on wineglasses and, in particular, with the development of the chandelier. Early glass examples were made in one piece and broke easily. A key advancement in chandeliers in the mid-eighteenth century was the use of separate, removable arms that could be replaced if broken. Every grand home now wanted lavish chandeliers for the ballrooms, and facet cutting meant that the light of the

A magnificent hanging chandelier, probably Irish, c.1780-90. This was originally exported to Russia and brought back to Ditchley Park, Oxfordshire. This masterpiece of construction is 3ft.3in. (1m) in diameter with a drop of approx. 5ft.6in. (1.7m).

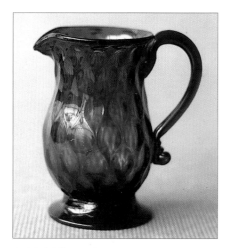

A delightfully simple blue glass cream jug with honeycomb moulding, early 19th century. Blue glass of this type is always associated with Bristol, but was made in many other centres including the United States. Firm attributions are usually impossible, but this example was purchased in America. 3½in. (9cm).

Recognising Irish glass relies on specific shapes and patterns of cutting, particularly in the field of decanters, the study of which is assisted greatly by marked specimens.

The chronology of the British decanter follows on from the wine bottle. Early glass bottles were used not for storage but for serving wine at the table, their round shape designed to assist with rapid cooling when placed in ice. Only wealthy homes used bottles made of clear glass. Around 1730 the so-called 'cruciform' shape became standard, the straight body moulded with deep flutes to maximise the surface area and increase cooling. Tall necks acted as handles to hold the decanters and lift them out of the iceboxes or cellarettes. By the mid-eighteenth century bottles became cylindrical to assist with storage, while decanters reverted to the 'globe and shaft' shape with a round body and slender tube neck. Stoppers were plain beaded balls, or sometimes pointed pear shapes. Very occasionally engraving was used to match sets of wineglasses with emblems such as Jacobite roses.

Classical elegance saw the round body give way to a shouldered shape, the body wider at the neck than the base. This was followed around 1775 by a bell or mallet shape tapering outwards to the base. Sometimes cutting was used and decanters would reflect the light from table candlesticks, and very occasionally a wine label would be engraved on the shoulder in place of the silver or enamel wine labels then in use. With cutting, decanters were naturally heavy and with the Excise Acts it is hardly surprising that Ireland became the centre of decanter manufacture.

Moulded techniques had been used in Bristol for making heavy, dark wine bottles before 1800. Similar methods were soon afterwards introduced to Ireland for the making of more delicate table glass. With great care, clear glass was blown into moulds to cast thin decanters, their shape closely following cut

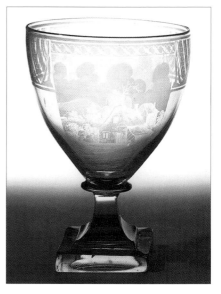

The Davenport factory, famous for its porcelain, also made glass in the 19th century. This square-based rummer is decorated by a curious process involving finely powdered glass paste fired on the surface, a technique patented by Davenport. c.1810. 10in. (25.5cm).

An early 19th century decanter with typical proportions. This has a triple annular ring neck and mushroom stopper. When the body is cut with fine diamonds it is important that it has not chipped badly on the points, as this spoils the glittering reflections. 9in. (23cm).

One of a pair of 'magnum' decanters with twice the capacity of normal decanters. These examples, probably from Ireland, have the unusual feature of coloured panels painted with figures representing Asia and Africa. Enamelling was popular on the Continent, but was rarely used in England or Ireland. c.1820. 13¼in. (35cm).

glass of the time, with trailed neck rings crudely added. The bases were moulded with bands of fine reeds or vertical facets to simulate the cutting previously added with a wheel. These basal flutes were important as the new thin, clear decanters showed up the sediment which remained in the bottom of most wines even after decanting. Moulds, of course, allowed glassmakers to add their names on the bottoms of their products for the first time. Decanters bearing the marks of 'Cork Glass Co.' or 'Penrose, Waterford' are

highly prized, but watch out for fakes. Jugs, finger bowls and 'wine coolers' or rinsers were made using the same moulds, but these were very rarely marked.

Other apparently unique shapes of glass

A typically Irish shape of fruit bowl, with 'turn-over' rim and a moulded, fluted 'lemon squeezer' base. Oval fruit bowls were heavy and so most examples surviving from this period were made in Ireland. c.1800. 13¾in. (35cm) long.

Irish cut glass items could have several uses. This base for a large punchbowl could be turned upside down and used as a dish-stand. It could also be used as a stand for a pineapple, or even a ham as part of a luxurious table setting. Early 19th century. 6⅞in. (17cm) diameter.   Sandon collection

vessel developed in Ireland. A series of very distinctive bowls were made with 'turn over' rims, the overhang intended to prevent chipping. On the other hand, bowls of elegant boat shape were given delicate rims cut with 'fan' or 'Vandyke' shapes that were very prone to damage. A third shape of round bowl has become known as a 'kettledrum' bowl. The bases are always robust and steady, either with step cutting or moulded underneath with a 'lemon-squeezer foot', so-called because of their resemblance to Victorian pressed glass kitchen utensils. Lemon-squeezer feet occur on many rummers and smaller wineglasses, as well as on a series of table salts that follow the same shapes as full sized boat-shaped bowls. Salts were often very heavy for their size and to avoid duty it would be natural for such objects to be made in Ireland. It would be unsafe to claim an Irish origin for every heavy moulded object, however. Piggins for cream, and certain distinctive shapes of light fitting are usually accepted as Irish more or less without question. Magnificent sets of oval dishes and plates with brilliant cut prisms will also probably be from Ireland if datable before 1825, for in that year the Excise Act was amended to include Ireland and the tax advantages came to an end.

Irish glass was not only exported back to England, for great quantities were shipped to Europe and to the United States where they proved to be very popular. Typical shapes of Irish decanters were copied in Bohemia and in Spain using cheap soda metal, and similar types were also made in Northern England. There is a tradition to call some lightweight spirit decanters Newcastle, but most are in fact Bohemian. Often these were given ornament using a thin 'flashing' of ruby glass at a time when little red glass was used in England.

When the Irish industry began to decline, many Irish workmen emigrated to America and took their mould-making skills with them. By this time there was already a flourishing glass industry in New England. Back in the 1760s a German, Henry Stiegel, had established a glassworks in Mannheim, Pennsylvania making lead glass, and among other German settlers John Amelung, who came from Bremen, made glass at New Bremen in Maryland. Stiegel employed Lazarus Isaac from Bristol as a cutter and engraver and in 1774 Isaac set up on his own when Stiegel closed his works. Only a few pieces can be attributed with certainty to Stiegel or Amelung and these are priceless treasures of Americana, for most early American glass sadly cannot be distinguished from the everyday German and Dutch glassware it copied so closely. Some of the moulded glass of early America is once again very difficult to identify for its similarity to Irish work.

English and Irish cut glass was generally superior in Europe at the end of the eighteenth century and was imitated, especially in France where locally made cut glass was referred to as 'façon d'Angleterre'. In Liège a substantial industry developed making glass with shallow

An Irish glass piggin used for serving cream, cut with fine diamonds below a prismatic band and a milled rim, the handles with fan cutting. c.1820. Piggins are traditional Irish shapes.

slice cutting in the English manner. Liège glass was generally inferior, sometimes with a slight yellow or green cast, and with bubbles and other impurities. Even so, many oval or round dessert baskets and stands, and pairs of classical shaped lidded urns for mantelpieces, offered for sale today as Irish or Waterford, originated instead in Belgium. Notwithstanding, they can be elegant decoration and generally are inexpensive considering their two centuries of age.

The superior skills of the top glasscutters working in Birmingham, Stourbridge and in London in the early 1800s produced highly desirable glass in spite of the cost. Full table services cut with patterns of graduated diamonds and highly refractive sharp flutes were used in grand houses and were the envy of foreign guests. In France and in Belgium English cutters were engaged to teach their skills and to work for the best glass decorating firms, including L'Escalier de Cristal in Paris, and Cappelmans of Brussels as well as at Val St Lambert. In France glass was treated as a precious material and cut glass vases or caskets were mounted in brightly gilded ormolu for added richness. In Russia decoration with cut glass was taken a stage further by the Imperial Glassworks in St Petersburg. Monumental vases were made from sections of glass joined with ormolu of unrivalled quality, and in 1828

A room in the Peterhof Palace set with table glass made for Tsar Nicholas I by the Imperial Glassworks in St Petersburg, c.1845-50. Russian cut glass was always of the highest quality.

(Opposite) A selection of fine Regency cut glass table lustres, hung with prismatic cut drops that reflect and sparkle as they gently sway in the candle light. The skills of the metal worker and glasscutter are exquisitely combined together. c.1820. Largest pair 13⅜in. (34cm) high.

the Shah of Persia was presented with a suite of Imperial Russian glass furniture.

Fashion changed across Europe and the popularity of fine diamond cutting gave way to a gentler but equally dramatic style. In France this is seen in the emerging opaline production, using stark shapes and vibrant colours. In Vienna glass beakers were equally abrupt in form, reflecting the Biedermeier style, and now used colour to create a very different effect. England was slow to discover colour in ornamental glass. Instead Britain's answer to Biedermeier was a new kind of cutting used on clear glass jugs and decanters. 'Broad flutes' were plain vertical facets or pillars, cut in sharp contrast to the fancy diamond patterns that had enjoyed such popularity. The new cutting style probably originated in Birmingham around 1820 and during the next two decades was used extensively.

One practitioner of the broad fluted style was Apsley Pellatt who now ran the Falcon glassworks in London. He needed strong but plain shapes to set off his invention – sulphides or 'cameo encrustations'. White clay portraits or sulphides had been used first in Paris, but Pellatt took out a patent in 1819, intending to use the technique in ambitious projects. Cameo heads were used in plaques and paperweights (see Chapter 9) as well as for decoration in

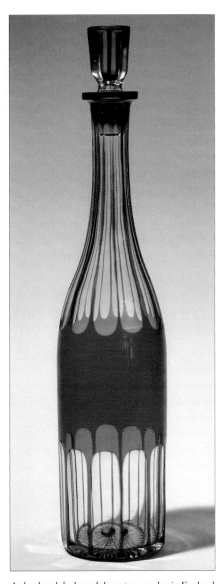

A cut glass scent bottle by Apsley Pellatt, containing a 'sulphide' of Captain James Cook. Pellatt & Co. patented their famous Crystallo Ceramie *or 'cameo incrustations' in 1819, a difficult technique copied later in France. c.1825-30. 4in (10cm). (Stopper lacking.)*

panels on the side of decanters or set in the centres of cut glass plates. The presence of sulphide plaques enables a few pieces of Apsley Pellatt glass to be identified. Aside from these, only a small number of documentary cut glass items listed in old museum collections can be ascribed to individual makers. While the top porcelain manufacturers of the day proudly marked their rich productions, the glassmakers did not. How frustrating that some of the finest British glass of all time – Regency cut glass – is destined to remain anonymous.

Further reading

Delomosne and Son Ltd., *Gilding the Lily*, Exhibition Catalogue, 1978

Charles Hajdamach, *British Glass 1800-1914*, Woodbridge 1991

Barbara Morris, *Victorian Table Glass and Ornaments*, London 1978

W. Phelps Warren, *Irish Glass*, London 1981

Hugh Wakefield, *Nineteenth Century British Glass*, London 1982

A slender club shaped decanter popular in England in the mid-19th century. These were often sold in sets of three in different colours, as the fashion for coloured glass arrived from the Continent. This example has a thin overlay of ruby (or cranberry) glass that has been cut with flutes around the shoulder and base. 16⅛in. (41cm).

CHAPTER 8

The Discovery of Colour

The colourful glass of Bohemia was a refreshing distraction amidst the political turmoil that was nineteenth century Europe. The end of the Napoleonic Wars had heralded a period of peace and prosperity in the Austrian Empire. New wealth was distributed widely among the middle classes who were free to combine an enjoyment of music, art and poetry with a comfortable home life. Instead of inherited furniture, the affluent bourgeois citizens of Vienna wanted everything to be new, made by craftsmen and finished to the highest standards. The Biedermeier interior was born from a desire to be different. Furniture was strong, loud and indelicate, polished to perfection or wrapped in textured veneers. Very different china and glass was needed to suit such furniture, and in Bohemia it was the Vienna State porcelain factory that led the way.

Topographical painting was one of the jewels of Austrian porcelain. In Vienna the decorator Anton Kothgasser had painted views of Vienna in coloured enamels on the white glaze of porcelain cabinet cups, and had learnt how to apply tooled gold borders to frame the scenes. Similarly Gottlob Mohn had learnt the technique of painting in enamels from his father, Samuel, a china painter from Leipzig who had decorated glass with portraits and silhouettes. Instead of the opaque enamels used on porcelain, Gottlob Mohn and Anton Kothgasser both perfected the use of transparent enamels which sat delicately on the surface of plain glass beakers, and in the case of Mohn, on very elegant decanters. The effect was rather like stained glass but with incredible detail. Views of Vienna, Dresden, Berlin and other towns and cities, carefully painted on flared tumblers, made ideal souvenirs bought by tourists travelling through Europe. Mohn's delicate painted scenes were combined with pretty borders of flowers or vines, while Kothgasser preferred to use bright gold on top of a pale amber wash. The Kothgasser workshop, established as an independent decorating studio in 1816, favoured a shape of strongly flared tumbler with heavily cut base known as a *Ranftbecher*. His signature, or the letter K, was sometimes hidden amongst the facets of the base cutting where it can be easily overlooked.

A Dresden beaker painted in 1811 with the Brandenburg Gate by the important glass decorator Gottlob Mohn who painted a series of similar beakers with German views for the Duke of Mecklenburg. Topographical painting was enjoying popularity on porcelain at that time and a small number of talented painters turned their attention to glass using transparent enamels. 4in. (10cm).

A Viennese Ranftbecker *painted in transparent enamels by Anton Kothgasser. The border of pansies, a pun on the French* pensé, *makes an appropriate lovers' gift accompanied by a suitable verse inscribed around the centre. Kothgasser had learnt skilful gilding at the Vienna porcelain factory. c.1820. 4⅜in. (11cm).*

A Bohemian engraved beaker with a detailed rendition of 'The Last Supper', possibly the work of Anton Simm. The established tradition of fine wheel engraving continued in Bohemia throughout the 19th century. c.1830. 5in. (12.8cm).

Other enamellers worked in Bohemia, including Carl von Scheidt who painted costumed figures and chinoiserie subjects (see page 48). In Haida, Friedrich Egermann experimented with coloured enamels and perfected a method of staining the surface of cut glass goblets using a thin layer of amber-yellow or deep ruby red. This process, generally referred to as 'flashing', created apparently solid pieces of rich red or amber glass. The important application of this process is discussed below, but meanwhile Egermann is famed for his other great invention, 'Lithyalin' glass, which he patented in 1829. This really developed from marbling techniques used in ancient Rome and in Venice, but the range, depth and control of colour now achieved pays tribute to Egermann's incredible genius.

The best-known colour of Lithyalin is a bright red, the colour of sealing wax, but it occurs also in all sorts of shades from grey to green, blue and purple. Beakers were created by careful blowing, mixing different batches of glass together, and applying heat with much precision to specific parts of the vessel. Finally the surface was cut and polished as if it really was banded agate or marbled malachite. Gilding was used to add a final richness to very costly but greatly prized pieces of glass, their style mirroring precisely the Biedermeier furniture.

Egermann's glass was soon imitated, not only in Bohemia but also in France at St Louis and elsewhere. At Count von Buquoy's glassworks in Southern Bohemia Lithyalin

An incredible example of a Bohemian glassmaker combining different techniques. Clear glass has been overlaid in amber and then cut and reticulated. The front panel has been engraved through the amber layer with a scene of an Arab and his horse, while the interior has been lined with silver to reflect light through the engraving. c.1840-50. 16in. (40.5cm).

was moulded with intricate gothic designs (see page 136). Some of Buquoy's Lithyalin glass possibly pre-dates Egermann's patent. Buquoy is rightly credited with the invention of 'Hyalith', a solid black glass he patented in 1817. This was used for beakers as well as cups and saucers gilded with flowers or Chinese figures.

When attributing Bohemian Lithyalin and Hyalith, it is important to look at the quality of the polished finish as well as the shape and style. While the fashion for marbled glass in the 1830s lasted only briefly, glass of similar appearance was made later, in France and in Russia in the 1890s, and again in Bohemia and elsewhere in the 1920s when moulded dressing-table sets and perfume bottles imitated malachite and other hardstones. Also, many vases and scent bottles made in a form of Lithyalin marbled in brown and sealing wax red colours originate in China. The dating of these Chinese Lithyalins is uncertain, for while some appear to be nineteenth century, many snuff bottles and vases are clearly of recent date.

Egermann's development of coloured 'flashing' had enormous implications for the Bohemian glass industry, for it transformed glass engraving. Fine engraving using a copper wheel had continued in Germany throughout the eighteenth century and now found an important centre in Bohemia. The skills were taught from father to son, and many independent glass decorating workshops were family concerns. Probably the finest independent engraver was Dominik Bieman who had trained as a portrait painter before joining the Pohl family to learn how to engrave glass. Bieman settled in Prague and earned valuable commissions from noblemen engraving portraits of their families. During the summer months he travelled to the favourite spa town of Franzensbad where he engraved portraits of visiting tourists as well as local views. The Biedermeier lifestyle gave the middle classes an opportunity for recreation, and the spa towns of Bohemia became crowded holiday resorts during the summer. Glass tumblers or beakers, for drinking the spa waters, made popular souvenirs and glass engravers set up workshops in most of the resorts.

Dominik Bieman and other superb engravers such as Anton Simm, Karl Pfohl and August Bohm, preferred to execute their art on colourless glass. Once Egermann's process of ruby flashing was in general use, however, the public wanted colour. Views of the spa buildings, town halls, hotels and even the railway stations were engraved into endless souvenir beakers, mugs or steins, through flashings of ruby, amber or occasionally blue. The beakers were frequently cut to leave a plain panel into which the owner's name and a date could be cut to make the souvenir more personal. The quality of these renditions varies greatly and while some can be beautifully detailed, others have a truly amateur feel. Spa beakers are plentiful today and generally inexpensive.

The other great pastime in Germany and Bohemia was hunting boars or stags, and the ideal way to recall a memorable hunting trip was to buy a fine covered glass goblet. Engraving shops earned a good living producing large numbers of such trophies, often beautifully engraved with stags and other deer resting in woodlands, or more animated scenes of huntsmen on horseback pursuing their quarry. These enjoyed great popularity until the 1850s when revolution threatened the peace in central Europe. Many engravers sought employment abroad, emigrating with their families to England and also to the United States. Several talented Bohemian glassworkers settled in Stourbridge where they were to transform the English glass industry (see Chapter 11).

Meanwhile during the 1830s experiments in Bohemia produced new and exciting colours and new techniques. Joseph Riedel is said to have named his invention of glass coloured with uranium after his wife, Anna. Consequently the wonderful, almost fluorescent, yellowish-green glass made in Bohemia and subsequently copied across Europe is referred to as 'Annagrun'. Riedel worked on his invention and perfected a more yellow version called 'Annagelb'. The dangerous nature of uranium wasn't appreciated in the

Stag hunting and horses were the two great recreations in Germany and these feature repeatedly on engraved Bohemian glass. The designs are individually cut on a wheel without any moulded outline. c.1850-60. 17⅛in. (43.5cm).

1830s as the curious colour enjoyed widespread popularity.

The process of flashing produced only a thin covering of coloured glass. 'Casing', on the other hand, allowed a bubble of one colour glass to be blown inside another differently coloured bubble. Initially outer layers of blue or red were cased on to clear glass vases or beakers which were then cut with geometric or leaf patterns. By 1830 it was possible to overlay one opaque colour on top of another, and finally after 1836 two or more different colours could be cased or 'overlaid' on to a base colour. The 1840s and '50s saw the creation of quite incredible examples of overlay glass, requiring the combined labours

A French opaline vase successfully imitating porcelain, painted in coloured enamels and edged with gold just like a china vase from Limoges. c.1890. 20½in. (52cm).

of many skilled glassworkers. Cutting wheels removed outer layers, or else they polished away the background to leave panels of the outer casing standing in relief. These panels could be enamelled with flowers, scenes or portraits that were then framed in gold to produce lavishly decorative sets of vases or pairs of perfume bottles.

The splendour of coloured overlay, and other clever uses of colour, spread the fame of

Many magnificent covered goblets were made in Bohemia in the middle of the 19th century, giving employment to hundreds of glass engravers. The most popular colour was ruby, for the thin red outer layer was simple to cut through and reveal the clear glass underneath. c.1850. This example stands 20¼in. (51.5cm).

French glassworkers' experiments with colour led to the development of many new 'opalines'. Here, a small cup in gorge de pigeon *is surrounded by a selection of milk white opaline with gilded decoration by Jean-Baptiste Desvignes, all c.1820.*

Bohemian glass all over the world. Bohemian workmen were attracted by offers of high wages to sell their secrets to foreign powers. Flashed and engraved glass, with various overlay patterns, was produced in Russia, in Belgium and especially in France where local makers were heavily rewarded for successful imitations of Bohemian glass.

Previously, 'Opaline' dominated coloured glass in France. Unlike the old Venetian milk glass that was totally opaque, French glass-makers preferred a form of semi-translucent, milky white glass that could be delicately coloured. The addition of bone ash to the glass mix resulted in the 'fire' for which opaline is famed, causing the colour of the glass objects to change when held to the light. White opaline glass was perfected around 1810 and gradually

more exotic colours were added to the repertoire including rich turquoise, a delicate amethyst, soft yellow and green. The most celebrated colour, a rose pink known as *gorge de pigeon,* glowed blood red from the fiery opaline deep within. The shapes favoured in France under the Empire were stark, classical forms, with plain surfaces to show the colour to best effect. It was left to the ormolu mounts to provide decoration, the tooled metalwork brightly gilded and adorned with the heads of eagles or swans. Around 1820 some opaline was decorated in gold and silver by Jean-Baptiste Desvignes, and gradually cutting of broad flutes and diagonal panels added slight ornament. Once Bohemian coloured glass became popular in France in the 1830s, plain opaline rapidly declined. The same French

Raised gold and silver add richness to a pair of Bohemian covered vases in brilliant blue glass, a style that found particular favour with Middle Eastern customers. c.1850. 15¾in. (40cm).

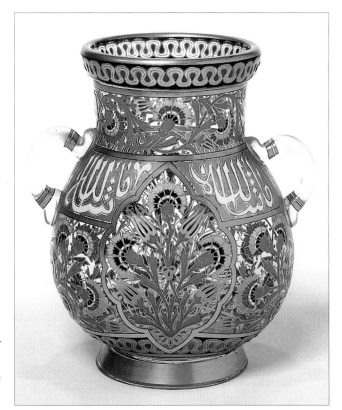

The decoration of old Islamic mosque lamps inspired this Lobmeyr vase sold in fashionable Vienna. Bright raised enamels and brilliant gold make no attempt to fake the appearance of a 12th century original, for this was a modern revival of the highest quality. Lobmeyr mark in white enamel, c.1875. 6¼in. (17cm).

colours were now adorned instead with gilded scrollwork and painted flowers.

Of course, copying took place the other way round, as some of the French opaline glass colours were made in Bohemia, and a range of opaline and opaque white glass was exhibited in St Petersburg in 1829. The later Viennese glass retailer and manufacturer, Lobmeyr, produced milky white opaline with careful enamelling, while in England opaque white and opaline glass was made after 1845 when the industry underwent radical change. The Glass Excise Act was finally repealed, and at last British manufacturers were allowed to experiment with new processes and materials. Experienced Bohemian workmen brought with them the techniques of casing and cutting

overlay glass, while painters and gilders from English porcelain factories moved to Stourbridge to help with decoration.

In the absence of makers' marks, it is frustrating to view superb examples of Victorian overlay glass and not know whether they originated in Bohemia, France, England or America. Pieces recorded in old museum inventories are testament to the problems of attribution, for products known to have been made by Bacchus of Birmingham, by Stevens and Williams and by Richardsons of Stourbridge look identical to glass exhibited at the 1851 Great Exhibition by French and Bohemian makers.

This enigma is particularly true of opaque white opaline vases. Popular around 1850,

Glass lithophanes tested the skill of the finest Bohemian engravers who could cut through incredibly thin layers of coloured glass. To produce the desired effect required remarkable precision, for the whole panel is no thicker than a window pane. c.1840.

Many old Venetian techniques were revived in the 19th century. This cracquelé *'Ice Glass' ewer was probably made in France around 1850 as part of a lemonade set with matching tumblers. 12¼in. (31cm).*

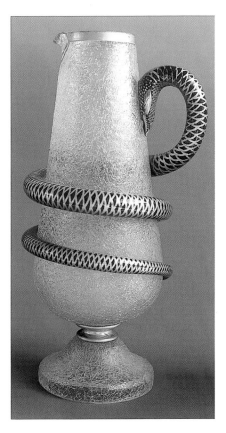

plain white vases were painted with colourful flowers, or fancy birds in exotic foliage, and these are always unmarked. It is fashionable to call such vases French, but we know many will be Bohemian or English. The firm of W.H., B. and J. Richardson of Stourbridge developed a good opaque white glass that was either painted or decorated for the first time with transfer prints. Richardsons also made clear glass painted in transparent enamels, especially a fine series of water jugs painted with irises or water lilies. Thankfully research has been carried out into surviving archives of British glass firms and gradually, instead of assuming a Bohemian origin, more and more credit is going where it deserves.

In the second half of the nineteenth century, Bohemia looked to the export trade and mass-produced coloured glass for shipment all over the world. Pairs of vases were produced either in a single colour opaque glass or in two-colour cased glass, and these were decorated with thickly enamelled flower subjects painted with great speed. Others were decorated with coloured lithographic prints copying famous paintings. Made in quantities in big factories, sets of these vases were available by mail order from catalogues of household goods throughout Europe, America and the Antipodes where they sold cheaply and in great numbers. These cannot be claimed as works of fine art, but they served their purpose well, providing inexpensive orna-

Historismus is an outrageous Victorian style inspired by mediaeval German art. This charger, made by Anton Egerman in Haida for the Viennese retailer Lobmeyr, is inspired by 16th century humpen, *while the ewer by Moser of Carlsbad depicts a very romanticised mediaeval knight. Note the tiny glass acorns applied to this ewer, for these occur on many Moser artefacts. c.1880-90. Charger 17⅛in. (43.5cm).*

ments to brighten up ordinary homes.

Long-established Bohemian makers such as Egermann continued to make glass aimed at a different market. Several other high quality Bohemian glassmaking firms including Ehrenfeld, Moser, Meyr's Neffe and Lobmeyr of Vienna joined them. The prevailing style in the 1870s-90s was *Historismus,* a confusing term that relates to a revival of traditional German vernacular ornament. Mediaeval, Gothic and Baroque motifs were combined together in a totally mixed-up way typical of Victorian times. Mediaeval chalices and reproduction *Humpen* and *Roemers* were copied

using bright colours that would have been quite out of place in the sixteenth and seventeenth centuries. While some carried spurious old dates, these were not made as fakes for they were sold openly in stores selling modern designs to suit the same revivalist taste in home interiors. Lobmeyr specialised in reproducing old glass, including fine 'rock crystal' engraving, *schwarzlot* painting in black enamel, and especially Islamic ornament copied from painted and gilded mosque lamps. Moser, an important glass firm in Carlsbad, specialised in raised enamelling on coloured glass, and they are best known for a pattern of colourful oak leaves to which were applied tiny moulded glass acorns.

As a field for collectors, colourful nineteenth century glass spans different national boundaries and a wide range of tastes, from pure Biedermeier and Empire to often very vulgar *Historismus*. Today it appeals to a wide audience, especially in the Middle East where much of it found a market originally. Bohemian glass is not an easy area for study,

not least because of the preponderance of fakes. Traditional Bohemian designs continued to be made into the twentieth century in Czechoslovakia and Poland, where overlay and cut glass beakers and vases are still made today. The copies are very rarely faithful to the elegant proportions of the originals, and the workmanship hardly ever comes close; for in terms of general quality, old Bohemian cutting and engraving can never be equalled.

Overlay glass involves one coloured layer cut away to reveal a different colour underneath. Such pieces are traditionally called 'Bohemian' for much overlay glass was made there, but the technique was also popular in France, and indeed in England too, made by immigrant Bohemian glassworkers. c.1850-70. Larger bottle 13⅜in. (34cm).

Bohemian glass from the Art Nouveau period but rather more traditional in its enamelled decoration of flowers with raised gold leaves, made by Moser and other makers, c.1890-1900. Largest vase 14⅛in. (36cm). Such pieces are decorative and yet out of fashion and consequently not expensive.

Further reading

Y. Amic, *L'Opaline Française au XIXe Siècle,* Paris, 1952

Olga Drahotvà, *European Glass,* London and New York 1983

G.E. Pazaurek, *Gläser der Empire und Biedermeierzeit,* Leipzig, 1923

Zuzana Pestova, *Bohemian Engraved Glass,* London 1968

S. Petrova and J-L. Olivié, *Bohemian Glass,* Paris 1990

Ada Polak, *Glass, Its Makers and Its Public,* London 1975

CHAPTER 9

Paperweights and Novelties

While theoretically most items of glass have a function, a great deal were never intended to be used. Very few vases have ever contained flowers and many colourful Bohemian beakers, too costly to fill with liquor, have spent their entire existence in a display cabinet. Paperweights were technically functional, for they could prevent your letters and papers blowing off your desk in a draught. In reality, though, most people bought paperweights purely for enjoyment, as frivolous novelties to sit there looking pretty.

There is no end to the fascination of glass paperweights – their brightly coloured tiny flowers or luminous bubbles creating kaleidoscopic effects guaranteed to mesmerise. Most paperweights encountered today are likely to have been made in Hong Kong where manufacture has always been cheap. Chinese paperweights are regularly brought along to The Antiques Roadshow, their proud owners hoping for good news on the value, but of course these can still be bought new for just a few pounds. The value of paperweights is all a question of quality, for when you put a pretty modern paperweight alongside an antique French one, there is usually no comparison. The incredible quality achieved in the Golden Age of paperweight manufacture – a mere fifteen years or so in the middle of the nineteenth century – has left us a rich heritage. The craft continues and many modern paperweights stand up well alongside the glories of the past.

Victorian paperweights really were a remarkable success story. Within just a year or two of their introduction sales had escalated and technology was advancing at an incredible rate. No one is sure where glass paperweights originated, for they seemed to appear in three different countries almost simultaneously.

Dates appearing on paperweights are curiously unreliable, but 1845 seems to be the earliest authenticated date on Venetian, Bohemian and French weights. I guess we shall never know who was copying whom.

The likely originator of the Venetian paperweight was Pietro Bigaglia. His paperweights were far from successful and appear to be true 'end-of-day' creations. In Venice fine millefiori and picture canes were set into glass panels and objects such as knife handles and desk seals. Ball-shaped paperweights were made containing irregular arrangements of odd canes left over, often broken and incomplete. Some contain the initials of Bigaglia who seems to have been unaware of the magnifying property of a clear glass dome placed above the canes. Picture canes in Venetian paperweights include local emblems such as the Lion of St Mark or gondolas, and even the head of the Pope. Rare and undoubtedly early in the story of paperweights, Venetian examples by Bigaglia are today surprisingly expensive considering their quality. Francini, another maker of early Venetian paperweights is best known for his many scent bottles containing picture canes and aventurine (sparkling gold dust). These interesting bottles are often let down by the poor quality of their metal stoppers.

Bohemia had led the world in experimentation using coloured glass (see Chapter 8) and it is likely that Friedrich Egermann worked on millefiori manufacture in an attempt to reproduce Roman mosaic glass. Balls of millefiori canes were in production in Bohemia by the mid-1840s and some of these were placed under clear domes for magnification. Apart from occasional signature letters, including a 'j' cane, the makers are unknown and the quality of Bohemian paperweights varies greatly. The best really are as good as

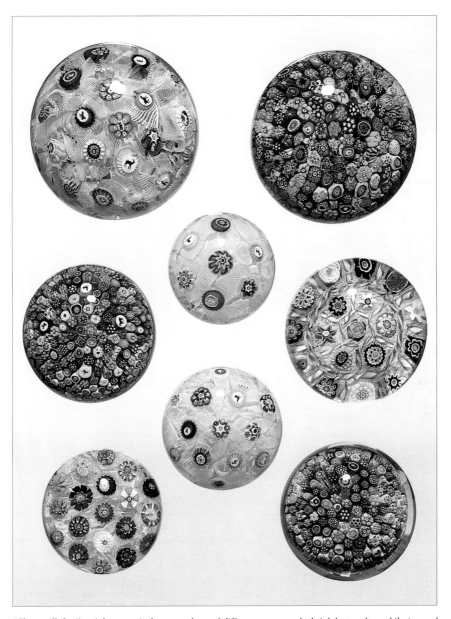

'Close millefiori' weights contain large numbers of different canes packed tightly together, while 'spaced millefiori' weights place single canes on 'upset muslin' grounds. Here Baccarat examples contain many distinctive 'silhouette' canes. The Clichy weight (centre right) uses lengths of turquoise 'barber''s pole' cable to divide the canes which are particularly well centred around a 'Clichy Rose'.

This St Louis 'Patterned' weight differs from conventional close millefiori by the inclusion of lengths of red, white and blue 'barber's pole', resulting in evenly divided panels around a perfectly centred composite cane. This skilful arrangement of beauty and rarity sold for £5,750 back in 1992.

The slightly awkward combination of a thistle, rose and pansy in this rare Clichy flat bouquet weight symbolises the alliance of Britain and France during the Crimean War. The formation of the rose petals is particularly characteristic and occurs as a cane in a great many Clichy weights.

A classic example of a Baccarat 'Flat Bouquet' paperweight. Baccarat flowers are not accurate botanical studies, but from within their glass bubble they bloom all year round with magnificent colours and a striking design.

anything from France, but these are the exceptions and many are disappointing.

While Bohemian and Venetian paperweights can only be regarded as failures, three principal glass manufacturers in France found success from the outset, for you do not find experimental or prototype versions of the standard French paperweights types. Millefiori weights containing the date 1845 have variously been ascribed to St Louis and Baccarat and they probably both started production at this time. Together with Clichy, these three makers dominate paperweight collecting, for their incredibly fine products speak for themselves.

Comparison is often made with sticks of seaside rock and this is a useful way to consider the creation of the individual 'canes' from which most paperweights are formed. Coloured glass patterns are stretched into incredibly thin rods and wherever they are sliced the full pattern is shown in the section. The most popular types are the 'cogwheel' and

Cutting is used to emphasise the three-dimensional quality of fine French paperweights. Here a Baccarat 'double overlay' patterned weight and a Clichy faceted 'concentric' weight flank a St Louis 'patch stand' with a distinctive 'crown' base.

'pastry-mould' canes, the names aptly describing their shape. 'Stardust' canes are made up of fine groups of tiny stars that look so pretty. Intricate canes provide important clues to the maker. Baccarat favoured a cane with little arrows arranged around the outside, known as an 'arrowhead' cane, while Clichy had the most distinctive cane of all. The 'Clichy Rose' resembles the head of a rose with layer after layer of curved petals, usually in pink and green. American and Bohemian makers copied the rose canes, but it is not difficult to recognise a true Clichy example.

The most interesting individual canes are silhouettes, made famous by Baccarat and St Louis. After moulding, these were stretched so that the animals seen in each cut section become amazingly small. Baccarat's 'close millefiori' paperweights contain all manner of silhouettes but you have to search hard to find the tiny dogs, horses, goats or monkeys hidden in the myriad of pattern canes. St Louis silhouettes

Snake weights were difficult to make and as a result vary greatly in their composition. This example uses a fine latticinio *ground and a central 'arrowhead' cane that confirms a Baccarat attribution.*

121

differ from Baccarat and assist in identification.

Individual makers sometimes signed their paperweights by including tiny initials in the design. Tucked in among Baccarat's canes can be found a letter 'B' and a date. 1847 and 1848 are the most usual dates encountered while 1846 and 1849 are rarer and so much more expensive. Other dates are incredibly rare, and this shows how short the great period of paperweight manufacture must have been. St Louis paperweights are sometimes initialled and dated, but Clichy very rarely signed. Any example signed 'Clichy' in full is worth a fortune, for values of course go hand in hand with rarity.

Pattern weights from France are amongst the most expensive, for the quality and detail can be exceptional. 'Concentric' paperweights have canes simply arranged in rings. 'Mushroom' paperweights are similar but the canes are raised up in a dome spreading from a tiny base. Other canes are formed into inter-laced 'garlands', while some have every centimetre of the design packed with tiny but perfectly formed canes, looking like a fine woven carpet. The important thing to consider is how well the canes are arranged, for a paperweight with misshapen or off-centre canes will be worth far less than a true example. The really finest paperweights can now command upwards of £50,000 ($80,000), such is the strength of the international market.

Fruit and flower paperweights are formed by 'lampwork', using a similar technique to the glassblowers who make glass animals at the end of a seaside pier. Skilled craftsmen form flowers by melting coloured glass rods together, and these are encapsulated within domes of clear glass, magnifying the tiny creations. Baccarat made the best flower paperweights in the nineteenth century, and some are incredibly beautiful. The most common flower was the pansy, for in French the name itself is a message of love. These made suitable gifts for the desk of a loved one, a flower that would never fade. Some flowers look very real and a truly wonderful effect is created by a varied collection of French flower weights.

The high standards meant French paper-weights were expensive, and after only a few years the novelty had worn off. Sales were slow, and by about 1860 all of the principal factories had given up paperweight production. There have been occasional revivals, by Baccarat in the 1920s for example, but the industry had generally moved elsewhere, to America, England and Bohemia once more.

In The United States paperweights were made by a large number of manufacturers, and have been the subject of extensive study. Attributions are problematic, for many workmen moved from one maker to another. The New England Glass Co. in Cambridge, Massachusetts, produced paperweights from about 1850 until the late 1870s, under the supervision of Frank Pierre who had learnt paperweight making in France working for Baccarat. The New England Company produced a full range of millefiori, flower and fruit paperweights including double overlays, all inspired by France. Rather more unique were their three-dimensional fruit paperweights, models of apples or pears inspired by old Venetian glass fruit.

The rival Boston and Sandwich Glass Co. in nearby Sandwich, Massachusetts, produced many paperweights using almost identical canes and these can easily be mistaken for New England. At Sandwich the most important workman was Nicholas Lutz who had worked at St Louis and then spent two years at New England, before moving to Sandwich in 1869. Lutz specialised in flower weights, especially bright red poinsettias, and he may have made many of the distinctive baskets of fruit attributed to Sandwich.

Frank Pierre's assistant at New England, William Gillinder, left to work for other firms before establishing his own glassworks in Philadelphia in 1861. Gillinder's weights are somewhat individual and often of high quality. The Mount Washington Glass Works in New Bedford made other very fine American paperweights during the 1870s, including the famous 'Mount Washington Roses'. At Millville, New Jersey, three-dimensional flowers, principally rose and tulips, were set in balls of clear glass raised on pedestal bases, while many somewhat crude paperweights containing written mottoes were also made at

Millville. In addition, many other American firms including Steuben and Tiffany also made paperweights. Needless to say, very few American makers marked their products in any way, and a great deal of experience is necessary to tell them apart.

In England Apsley Pellatt had made cut glass ornaments containing sulphide portraits back in the 1820s, but the principal production of sulphide paperweights took place in France. Baccarat and Clichy included very fine detail in their sulphide portraits, and paperweights depicting Queen Victoria and Prince Albert were made in France and in America for sale in England. English makers attempted sulphides, and a number of reasonably successful 'pinchbeck' paperweights, with scenes cast in metal below a dome of clear glass, are believed to be English. It is significant that Continental paperweights first appeared in 1845, the same year that the Glass Excise Acts were relaxed and English glassmakers were finally free to experiment. As a result, two companies were soon actively involved in the manufacture of millefiori paperweights.

Bacchus and Co. of Birmingham were certainly producing paperweights by 1848 and were responsible for some rare but very well made examples. A curious feature of some Bacchus productions is the use of canes of very different sizes placed within a single paperweight. The Whitefriars Glassworks in London, operated by James Powell and Sons, made most of the paperweights attributable to England. Whitefriars paperweights actually show very little variety, for most are concentric patterns constructed from repetitive canes in a limited range of colours. Large in size, they often have a separate foot raising the outside of the paperweight. The quality of some English paperweights attributed to Whitefriars is disappointing, and it is now believed that other unknown makers were responsible for many of these. A great range of glass inkbottles was made containing paperweight bases, their stoppers set with matching miniature paperweights. The best of these are undoubtedly from Whitefriars, but other makers, probably in Stourbridge, produced similar millefiori inkbottles. Many Whitefriars

A cheap Victorian souvenir paperweight shaped as a bell filled with coloured sand from Alum Bay in the Isle of Wight. The picture, cleverly formed from tiny grains of coloured sand, shows a local landmark known as the Mumbles. 4⁷/₁₆in. (11.4cm).

Sandon collection

or Whitefriars-type paperweights contain dated canes, especially 1848, but these dates need to be treated with caution.

Paperweights were sold by stationers as well as by shops selling fancy goods. They became popular as presents to bring back from holidays, and gift shops naturally looked to the local souvenir market. Many people are surprised at the age of some souvenir paperweights. Visitors who admired the original French paperweights at the 1851 Great Exhibition bought inexpensive mementoes to take home, including pretty glass paperweights

Scenic view souvenir paperweights can date back to the middle of the 19th century. This scene of Chatsworth was printed directly on to the underside of the weight and coloured in by hand. 2½in. (6.5cm).
Sandon collection

An American souvenir paperweight sold to visitors at the Chicago Exhibition in 1893. Colour printing has now replaced hand colouring. 4in. (10cm).
Sandon collection

containing views of the exhibition buildings – the celebrated Crystal Palace in Hyde Park. These early scenic view paperweights used the magnifying property of the glass dome to show landmarks or hotel buildings printed on to the underside of the weight. The pictures were hand-coloured and flakes of mother-of-pearl were applied to represent water or windows.

Some were made in England or France, but most seem to be Bohemian.

The development of photography brought even cheaper scenic paperweights from about 1870, and colour printing was used after 1890. The earlier hand-coloured prints are more desirable, but avoid examples where the protective backing has been damaged and thus the picture has deteriorated. Inexpensive collections can be formed today, not only of scenic souvenirs but also the numerous kinds of advertising paperweights that were very popular in the United States up to the 1930s.

During the nineteenth century a rather different type of paperweight enjoyed great popularity in England. 'Dumps' or 'Dumpy' weights really were 'end-of-day' creations, for they were initially made using waste glass from bottle factories. Bubbles were trapped in solid masses of green bottle glass and sold for a few pennies around Northern English bottle factories. Dumps gradually caught on and were produced for general sale. Some of the trapped bubbles were manipulated with care into distinct patterns, and during manufacture finely powdered chalk was sprinkled to give the appearance of thin sheets of foil trapped within the green glass. Some dumps were of large size, intended as doorstops, although photographs of Victorian interiors show that they were also placed on mantelpieces as ornaments. Dumps were made wherever bottle factories were located. Many are associated with Stourbridge, but the best known maker is the firm of John Kilner and Sons of Wakefield, a bottle manufacturer famous as the maker of 'Kilner' storage jars. A few rare Kilner dumps can be identified by stamped maker's marks. Dumps containing crude sulphides of Queen Victoria for the 1897 Jubilee and Edward VII for his coronation in 1902 are rare datable specimens, but these aside it is very difficult to tell just when dumps were made. They are now popular with collectors once more and increasingly hard to find in good condition.

Following the decline of the French paperweights, Europe took a long time to attempt any revival. During the 1920s and '30s, many shapeless creations were made in

'Dumps' or 'Dumpy Weights' were traditionally made by workers in glass bottle factories to use up left over glass. Examples containing foil flowers are particularly desirable, but avoid specimens with surface bruises.

Czechoslovakia and today collectors generally ignore these. The Czechoslovakian millefiori paperweights were poor offerings, it is true; but some of their abstract glass ornaments, using trapped bubbles and spattering of colour, were very much ahead of their time. With careful faceting of the surface, some of these so-called 'Art Deco' paperweights deserve greater appreciation; but do not confuse 1920s Czechoslovakian paperweights with later copies made in China.

Since the Second World War there has thankfully been a revival of what was in danger of becoming a lost art. St Louis, Baccarat and Whitefriars reintroduced their old processes and by the 1960s they were once more making fine quality paperweights, mostly as limited

editions. In Scotland many superb paperweights have been made, in a tradition started in the 1920s by the great paperweight master Paul Ysart. Ysart developed new types of coloured background into which patterned canes and lengths of cable were carefully set, and within these patterns he created flowers, fish or butterflies. His best paperweights, made at Perthshire and in Caithness, were signed with the initials PY in a neat cane.

More recently in Scotland, superb paperweights in traditional style have been made by William Manson, John Deacons and others. Alongside these have been produced paperweights with a very different appearance – ultramodern conceptual creations with titles inspired by distant galaxies or spacecraft. Some abstract paperweights can be exciting and indeed, the best modern American examples are truly breathtaking.

Some modern American makers have been hailed as great artists and are collected as keenly as the best nineteenth century makers. Richard Ayotte specialises in birds with feathers that look real. Delmo Tarsitano places creepy but intriguing lizards among volcanic rocks. Bob and Ray Banford design formal

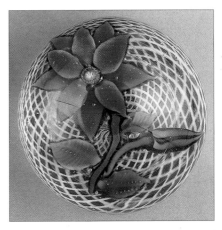

An American poinsettia weight in the manner of Nicholas Lutz who worked for the Boston and Sandwich Glass Co., c.1870s.

A modern Scottish 'swirl' paperweight by John Deacons, in traditional style and as yet not expensive, but of good quality. 2½in. (6.4cm).
Sandon collection

New abstract concepts in paperweight design were introduced in Scandinavia and Venice in the 1950s and were adopted universally. This example, which is superbly constructed, is by the American maker Bob Eickholt of Ohio and is dated 1987. Sandon collection

flowers and use overlay techniques and surface cutting to add to the excitement. Finally, the greatest of all modern makers, Paul Stankard, has produced flowers in glass so real you would swear a freshly picked specimen has been encased in molten glass. Stankard's flowers really have taken paperweight making into a new dimension, and the prices which they command at auction would please any investor, although once you own a Stankard paperweight you would never want to part with it.

Returning to the nineteenth century, paper-weights were only a very small part of a massive market in glass novelties. The continual increase in home ownership had created a valuable international trade in trinkets with no function other than to amuse. The fashion for big fireplaces in Victorian homes meant that larger mantelpieces cried out to be covered with ornaments. Unlike the dramatic but somewhat stark Biedermeier and Regency interiors, the fashion now was for rooms to be crammed with decoration. Colourful glass was of course highly decorative and there cannot have been many homes that did not possess at least one elaborate epergne or a pair of lustres

sparkling in the glow of new gas lighting.

Lustres had changed significantly from their forerunners, the cut glass candlesticks of the early nineteenth century. Colour had replaced clear glass, and the candle nozzles no longer functioned. Vase-like tops contained only the occasional dried flowers or silk bouquet. From Bohemia in the 1840s came cut glass lustres with coloured overlay or ruby and amber flashing. Painted flowers and bright gilding added to the effect in the middle of the century, and these were in turn replaced by opaque cased glass examples. During the 1880s and '90s lustres got bigger and bigger, cased in shocking colours such as strawberry pink and enamelled with crude sprigs and cheap gloss gilding. The suspended drops were cut with highly reflective patterns that sparkled as they swung. Victorians detested dust, however, and covered many lustres with glass domes that prevented the drops from swinging. Curiously, the somewhat vulgar 1880s lustres can be more expensive today than the higher quality over-lay and cut examples.

Epergnes were centrepieces for decorating a table. These too had prototypes in Regency England, formed from dishes and bowls of

A pair of table lustres hung with prism-shaped drops that reflect light as they swing and jangle together. These 'cased glass' examples were made in Bohemia and have enamelled decoration typical of the 1880s.

clear cut glass supported by elaborate silver constructions. The metal supports for Victorian epergnes were very much simpler brass fittings that held trumpet-shaped flower holders in coloured glass. Different numbers of flower-like glass horns rose up from the centre of flower bowls. The horns were interspersed with spiralling glass rods from which could be hung dainty glass baskets for further posies or for serving sweets. Fancy glass trailing, pincered while still molten, added to the decorative effect.

Epergnes were the speciality of Stourbridge and North-east England and came in various colours, especially 'cranberry', the North American name for light ruby glass. Others were made in yellowish-green uranium glass (see Chapter 8). Opaline-like milky shading was used within the coloured glass to create an effect called in England 'pearline', although today the American name 'Vaseline' is generally used instead, for uranium-coloured pearline glass closely resembles the oily sheen of vaseline. All manner of vase shapes were

Epergnes were created in many levels of complexity. This relatively simple American example with only four flower trumpets is formed of 'Amberina' glass shading from amber to deep cranberry. c.1890.

made in cranberry, vaseline and other coloured or patterned glass. Other popular shapes included sugar bowls and cream jugs, as well as decanters and full sets of drinking glasses and tumblers for everyday use. These were sold alongside the lustres and epergnes in fancy-goods shops together with other novelties that had no function other than to look pretty.

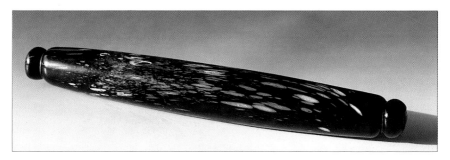

Rolling pins were initially functional objects used in kitchens in Northern England and they became popular as gifts in Victorian times. Today these can form an inexpensive collection. This example is from the early 19th century.

Glass bells, trumpets, hats and walking sticks were regarded as items of fun and bought as curiosities. Their origin was in fact a very real tradition associated with the glass factories of Britain. Each year the glassworkers took part in a trade procession through the streets of their town, carrying items made of glass to represent their skills. The tradition apparently began in the eighteenth century when workers carried dishes or decanters still joined on to their blowing tubes. To show off their fancywork, they began to decorate their costumes with cut glass drops or chains from chandeliers; then they wore glass feathers in their hats, and finally many workers took to wearing glass hats. They carried swords or walking sticks made from glass, and rang peals of glass bells. In Newcastle upon Tyne, or Warrington, friendly rivalry between the many local glass firms led to serious competition, each trying to out-do the others in their technical mastery. Entire suits of clothes were woven from threads of finely spun glass, and bands played in the processions, every one of their instruments from the bugles to the violins made out of glass. In some parts, the glass processions continued into the early twentieth century.

Nailsea, near Bristol was just one of many glassmaking towns where trade processions took place, but for some reason the name of Nailsea has become synonymous with the glass novelties carried in the processions. 'Nailsea' hats and bells, pipes and rolling pins, and shepherdesses' crooks, were in reality made all over

Britain. They were not all used in the processions, of course, and they were not all made just at the 'end-of-day' using up spare glass from the furnaces. Instead glass novelties were on sale at the factories all year round and were bought as popular gifts. Collectors today tend to specialise in a specific shape, and coloured novelties, especially in cranberry or deep blue, are more desirable than colourless examples.

Once upon a time glass bells were rung in processions by glassblowers, but by 1880 they had become popular as novelty ornaments. These cranberry bells are probably from North-east England.

Among the 'friggers' carried in the glass workers' processions were models of buildings or ships made out of glass. In Sunderland and Newcastle, in particular, glass ship models enjoyed great popularity and the largest of these, anything up to a metre high, are virtuosities of glassmaking. Fountains and grottoes included cascading waterfalls and peacocks with spreading tails, all made from finely spun glass. It is remarkable to think that the processes used to produce the fine strands of glass led eventually to today's' fibre-optic technology. Victorian friggers were created to fit under glass domes and without their original domes the ships with their amazing rigging have simply not survived.

Friggers and 'Nailsea' novelties are very British objects, but other fancy glass such as epergnes and lustres were also made in Bohemia and the United States. It is usually impossible to tell the origin of jugs, vases and other shapes in cranberry glass, for the workmen responsible often took their skills with them when they emigrated. Shapes and designs are often universal. 'Mary Gregory' glass will be forever associated with early American glass, for Mary Gregory herself was a worker at the Boston and Sandwich

'Friggers' are closely associated with Nailsea but in reality were made in many parts of Britain, especially the West Midlands. This particularly large example includes fountains, birds, animals and ships, all made entirely from trailed and spun glass. An original glass dome is essential.

'Mary Gregory' glass is hard to attribute as identical vases were manufactured in several countries. These typical large vases were probably made in Bohemia, c.1880-1900.

Glassworks in the 1880s where it is believed that she painted figures of children in white enamel on coloured glass pitchers. The first white-painted children were probably attempts at imitating Stourbridge cameo glass carved with figures by the Woodalls (see Chapter 11). Copies of English cameo were made cheaply in Bohemia and the popular sentimental pattern of boys and girls appeared in quantity from about 1885. These were copied in America and in England soon afterwards. Early books on collecting Victorian glass in America mentioned Mary Gregory as one of the decorators responsible, and her name quickly stuck. 'Mary Gregory' glass has therefore become a generic name and most of the treasured vases in America are likely to be Bohemian imports. They are, however, all keenly collected and as a

result it is necessary to watch out for the many fakes that are on the market.

Many new forms of fancy coloured glass were developed at the end of the nineteenth century and these have become known as 'art glass'. Stourbridge was the centre of experimentation by the three principal local firms of Webbs, Richardsons and Stevens and Williams (Royal Brierley). Corrosive chemicals were used to give coloured glass frosted or 'satin' finishes with the sheen of mother-of-pearl, and internal textures were created by manipulating trapped bubbles within the glass. Amongst Thomas Webb and Sons' most successful art glass was 'Peachblow', that shaded from deep red to pink, and 'Burmese', a frosted satin glass that shaded from pale primrose-yellow to delicate pink. Graduating the heat during manufacture created the shading. Burmese glass was used to make small posy vases and the shades of glass nightlights in particular, for when these were lit they gave a gentle rosy glow. The surface could be matt or shiny, and was sometimes painted in delicate enamels or decorated with raised-paste gilding, a technique perfected by Jules Barbe who worked for Webbs. Another unusual decorating technique known as 'coralene' involved attaching tiny glass beads to the surface using an enamel paste to create a wonderful glow when held in certain light.

Webbs had bought their patent to make Burmese glass from the American inventor, Frederick Shirley of the Mount Washington Glass Co. At the end of the nineteenth century America overtook England in the race to develop art glass. Many glassworkers from Stourbridge emigrated to America, including Joseph Locke who joined the New England Glass Co. Frederick Carder had helped to develop many of the most significant colours in new art glass at Stevens and Williams before settling in America where he founded the Steuben Glass Works at Corning (see Chapter 13).

Copying was widespread. Mount Washington tried to protect their rights to important inventions, including their 'Crown Milano' glass that imitated the ivory porcelain of Royal Worcester, but enforcing patents internationally proved very difficult. Not long after Burmese glass was in production at Mount Washington, copies were being made in other American factories and in Bohemia. Satin, coralene and many other forms of art glass were made cheaply in Germany and Bohemia, but these copies were usually much inferior to the originals. After years of neglect, Victorian art glass became enormously collectable during the 1960s. Values rose rapidly, but unfortunately the increased prices led to widespread faking once again. Nowadays,

'Queen's Burmese' glass was patented by Thomas Webb and Son and named after Queen Victoria. The delicate shading from pale primrose to deep rose pink was incredibly popular in the 1880s, especially for shades for fairy lights. This posy vase by Webbs has additional enamelling.

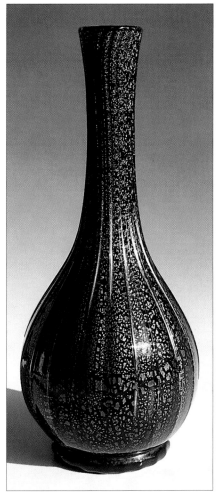

'Coralene' is a rare form of decoration applied to satin glass. The weed-like coral branches that sparkle in the light are formed from tiny glass beads set in yellow enamel. This example is probably American, c.1890.

English Art Glass can be adventurous and way ahead of its time. This 'Ribbed Rockingham Crystal' vase attributed to Stevens and Williams dates from around 1880 and anticipates techniques used later in Continental Art Nouveau. 14¼in. (36cm).

great care has to be taken as reproduction cranberry, Mary Gregory and satin glass turns up everywhere.

Further reading

Ray and Lee Grover, *Art Glass Nouveau,* Rutland, Vermont, 1967

Charles Hajdamach, *British Glass 1800-1914,* Woodbridge 1991

Paul Hollister Jr., *The Encyclopedia of Glass Paperweights,* New York, 1969

Paul Jokelson, *Sulphides,* New York 1968

James Mackay, *Glass Paperweights,* New York 1973

Patricia McCawley, *Antique Glass Paperweights from France,* London 1968

Sara Rossi, *Letts Guide to Collecting Paperweights,* London 1990

Keith Vincent, *Nailsea Glass,* 1975

CHAPTER 10

Moulded Glass

While we tend to think of moulded glass as a nineteenth century discovery, moulding is almost as old as glass itself. Clay cores were used to form Egyptian glass bottles, while the famed glassworker Ennion proudly signed some of the finest Roman coloured glass pieces formed using his detailed moulds. In this chapter we need to distinguish between two different moulded techniques – blown moulded glass and press moulding.

Venetian workmen continued the Roman method of moulding glass. A basic object was formed as a bubble on the end of the blowing iron and inserted inside a mould most likely made of iron. Further blowing caused the bubble to fill the mould, which was

An early example of decorative press-moulding attributed to Webb Richardson of Stourbridge, signed with initials WR. The background of tiny beads embossed on the underside produces a curious sparkling effect when viewed from the front of this colourless glass plate. c.1836. 6½in. (16.5cm).

Sandon collection

constructed in sections that could then be opened, and the formed object removed. Surprisingly, in sixteenth and seventeenth century Europe blown moulded glass was rarely as fine as the ancient Roman pieces. Venetian, Dutch and French factories experimented with what amounted to mass-production methods, but with little success. In France at Orléans in the later seventeenth century very clear glass was used to mould portrait medallions, while scent bottles were cast in several different colours including milk white to imitate porcelain. In England around 1700 serving bottles and decanters were blown into rough moulds to form octagonal bodies or the distinctive 'cruciform' shapes (see page 82). In the eighteenth century some wine-glasses were placed on moulded stems while bowls were sometimes ornamented with honeycomb, flowers or faceted patterns, usually with little definition.

Significant improvements in blown moulding occurred once much of the industry had moved to Ireland. Decanters bearing the moulded marks of the Cork Glass Company were beautifully thin, although the moulding was restricted to simple bands of flutes around the bases. Copies of the popular Irish decanters were made in Bohemia, Scandinavia and in particular in the United States and it is therefore very difficult to attribute unmarked examples. Early American factories saw moulding as a means to produce profitable cheap glass. This not only competed with European imports in the American market but in turn a lot of American glass was exported to Europe. During the 1820s and '30s blown glass flasks became a speciality of several American glass factories such as the Union Glassworks in Philadelphia and others in Pittsburgh and Kentucky. Flasks were produced in different patterns and colours including commemorative and patriotic subjects. Fragments of these distinctive flasks have been excavated on the sites of the American glass factories allowing identification and a detailed classification that is very important. Early American moulded flasks have been collected for a long time and high values have led to a proliferation of fakes, especially of the valuable coloured examples. Copies vastly outnumber genuine flasks and it takes much experience to tell the originals from the best of the fakes.

America didn't actually invent press moulding, although the process was used extensively in the United States from the 1820s onwards. Prior to this, in Bohemia and in Ireland at the end of the eighteenth century, table salts and the bases of bowls and wineglasses had been stamped or cast using metal moulds. Distinctive moulded feet on English or Irish rummers and turnover-rimmed bowls were produced in square shaped moulds into which a blob of molten glass was dropped. A special 'former', shaped very much like a lemon-squeezer, was pressed into the mould to push the glass into shape, and this in turn left a distinctive fluted dome hollowed out underneath the moulded feet. These so-called 'lemon squeezer' bases were then attached to large bowls, rummers or smaller salt containers. The process was awkward and surviving examples are frequently irregular.

Significant developments in the process of press moulding were introduced in America at the start of the 1820s. Special machines were developed to hold a heated metal mould in place while a measured amount of molten glass was dropped in straight from the firemouth. The mould formed the patterned underside of a plate or dish or the exterior of a bowl, while a smooth plunger would be squeezed down from above to fill the mould and leave the top or interior smooth and reasonably even. Skill was required to use just the correct amount of glass, and the temperature of the mould and the glass mix was also crucial so that the glass did not stick to the mould.

The success of pressed glass depended on

Simple mould-blown tumblers were made in France in the 17th century using the same techniques adopted in Ireland and the United States. Firm attributions and precise dating are therefore difficult, but this is probably American and early 19th century. 2½in. (6.2cm).   Sandon collection

maintaining detail after moulding. When pressed glass items were removed from the moulds they had an unpleasant rough texture on the surface. This was not too important when factories made copies of heavy cut glass patterns as moulded versions were expected to be cheap. With more delicate designs glassmakers disguised the surface wrinkles by developing patterns made up of small raised bead-like motifs. In the 1830s and '40s the so-called 'Lacy' patterns became very fashionable, but to be effective these still required crisp definition. After moulding, early pressed glass had to be 'firepolished' to become smooth. This meant placing the object back into the firemouth or into a separate furnace where the surface was re-melted, and inevitably this meant some of the detail was lost. Firepolishing also softened the sharp seams left by the joins in the mould. Glass squeezed between gaps in the mould left thin, sharp projections known as 'fins' and these had to be removed. Particularly bad seams were removed using cutting wheels but this added to the costs of what were essentially cheap items.

The ideal shape for manufacture using a glass press is a small plate, and it so happened that these were very popular items in America

A 'Lithyalin' cup and saucer moulded from marbled red, brown and black glass, probably made in France rather than Bohemia, c.1840-50. Glass-makers felt they could rival porcelain manufacturers but the quality of their early moulded glass teaware was unreliable.

An American pressed glass 'cup plate' on which a teacup was placed while tea was drunk from a saucer. Early American glassworks made a great many cup plates in so-called 'lacy' patterns. c.1840. 3½in. (8.7cm). Sandon collection

at the time. European families drank tea using handled cups placed on saucers, but in the United States it was usual to drink tea from the saucer. Tea was poured from the cup into the saucer and the empty cup was placed on a tiny plate called a 'cup plate'. European porcelain tea services did not include 'cup plates' and so in American homes pressed glass cup plates were used instead. These became the speciality of firms such as the Boston and Sandwich Glass Company where a great range of cup plates was made. Most were decorated with lacy patterns where the ground included raised dots or beads that sparkled through the coloured glass. Cup plates were popular as commemorative souvenirs and some illustrate the export trade to Europe, for among the designs that have been found on the site of Sandwich and other American glassworks are portraits of Queen Victoria, Prince Albert and emblems of the Prince of Wales. These date from around 1840 and were made to mark the coronation and wedding of Victoria and the birth of her eldest son. Many of the examples found in England seem to have originated in America, though the situation is further

complicated by Birmingham mould makers who supplied some of the moulds used by American and French glass factories.

American lacy pressed glass was soon copied in France, Bohemia and in England. Different glassworks bought their moulds from independent mouldmakers, and it was also usual for some factories to sell worn moulds to other minor producers. In France the large glassmakers – St Louis, Val St Lambert and Baccarat – all produced finely moulded glass, both clear and coloured. Moulded Opaline was made in France alongside Hyalith and Lithyalin glass and the same lacy designs, inspired by the fashion for Gothic ornament, were also made in Bohemia by Count Buquoy and at other glassworks. Attributing Continental pressed glass, such as the cup and saucer shown here, is therefore particularly difficult.

In England, the abolition of the Glass Excise tax in 1845 had a great impact on the manufacture of pressed glass. Firms were free to experiment and could now make heavy pressed dishes that sold cheaply. Metalworkers in Birmingham produced high quality moulds and the first British pressed glass was made locally and in Stourbridge. Progress was slow in England because glassworkers initially distrusted the new machines they felt

An American 'Slag' fruit bowl and two posy vases in 'malachite' and 'Sorbini' glass by Sowerby, just a few of the intriguing colour effects available in late Victorian moulded glass.

threatened their livelihood. There was, however, a huge market for simple domestic glassware and patterned pressed glass soon replaced plain tumblers in pubs and taverns. Facets and dimples, previously cut on a wheel, were now moulded to provide very inexpensive glassware for a new market. In early Victorian times the price of sugar fell sharply and glass cream jugs and sugar bowls were now used in workers' homes, imitating the habits of the middle class households.

Similarly, since the removal of tax on salt in 1835, this became another former luxury available to all. Moulded glass salts were produced in unbelievable quantities in mid-nineteenth century England and many survive. Costing relatively few pounds, moulded salts today offer great scope for collectors.

In due course the British glass industry moved to take advantage of cheaper labour and coal. Manchester and the North-east became the centres for the manufacture of pressed glass, made now in larger and larger factories. The two biggest were both in Gateshead, where the Tyne supplied access to the world export market. In 1850 John Sowerby moved his family's glassworks to a sew site in Ellison Street in Gateshead next to the railway station. The local unions objected to the use of machinery but Sowerby himself earned much respect from his workforce for his knowledge

of glassmaking and the many advancements he introduced. Output grew dramatically, until the 1880s when Sowerby's Ellison Glass Co., covering 5½ acres (2.2 hectares), was the largest factory in the world. Up to 1,000 workers produced 150 tons of finished glass articles every week, most of it exported.

In 1876 Sowerby's registered their mark of a peacock head crest. This was used on their 'Vitroporcelain', a form of opaque glass in a variety of pure single colours. The name was chosen to represent strength and the market with which it competed, for Sowerby's glass was cheaper than porcelain but just as durable. Milk white and bright turquoise were the most popular colours, while more exotic tints included 'Queens Ivory' made to compete with the ivory porcelain of Royal Worcester. Identical shapes were made in different colours and collectors particularly seek the rarest Sowerby colours – 'Rubine', a translucent red, opaque yellow and 'Aesthetic Green', an almost fluorescent colour inspired by Oscar Wilde and Gilbert and Sullivan.

Sowerby's pressed glass is often referred to as 'slag glass'. Slag, a waste product discarded by the local ironworks, was used in the mix for some colours but the resemblance between the marbled glass and iron slag is just coincidence. Sowerby called their green and white marbled glass 'malachite' and their marbled blue glass

A pair of busts of Gladstone and Disraeli. They are unmarked but may be by the maker John Derbyshire, c.1880. French makers such as Baccarat made successful portrait busts in colourless and frosted glass, but the English attempts, cast in luminous green, were far less successful.

'Sorbini', both rare colour effects much sought after today. The same shapes were made in every colour and today some collectors go for variety while others choose a shape and try to find it in as many different colours as possible. Many miniature baskets were made to hold posies of flowers. The same shapes were cast either open or with the handles folded in – pushed together while the glass was still

English bottle factories produced ornaments as cheap sidelines alongside bottle production. Moulds for cast iron mantelpiece dogs were adapted for use with molten glass, but much detail was lost. Mid-19th century.

malleable before annealing. John Sowerby's son, John George Sowerby, was an illustrator of children's stories and he probably introduced an important series of nursery rhyme patterns that are the most expensive of the Sowerby designs, especially when they occur in the rarer colours.

Noting the success of Sowerby's factory, another local businessman in 1867 set up a glassworks in competition. George Davidson's pressed glass manufactory, also in Gateshead, was smaller than Sowerby's, but still employed 350 workers and produced 200-250 tons of glass articles every month.

Davidson's range of colours was not as extensive as Sowerby's but included similar marbled glass. Much use was made of milk-white and jet-black coloured glass as well as translucent amber and light blue. Shapes were rarely adventurous, for Davidson decided to concentrate on sets of glassware in a smaller range of popular patterns, often copying cut glass designs such as his best-selling 'hobnail' design. Davidson's mark was also a family crest, that of a half-lion rising from a crown, used only during the 1880s.

Landseer's monumental lions at the foot of Nelson's Column inspired these cheap moulded glass versions intended as paperweights. The same models were produced in ranges of colours, creating interesting opportunities for collectors, North-east England, c.1880.

Amongst Davidson's specialities are commemorative wares for popular events like the Queen's Jubilees, and a distinctive colour effect in his moulded glass known at the time as 'pearline'. After moulding in pale blue or in yellow translucent glass, the pearline effect was created by returning the glass object to the firemouth and rapidly heating the rim. This caused a chemical change whereby the rim turned opaque white. Davidson's Pearline was introduced in 1889 and enjoyed great success in overseas sales.

The third of the great British pressed glass factories was established on Wearside at Sunderland. Henry Greener and Co.'s factory was never on the same scale as its Tyneside rivals, but it still produced a vast output of fancy glass in an impressive range of colours and patterns. In line with Davidson's, commemorative plates were again produced in numbers, and many of Greener's top-selling patterns copied popular cut glass designs including the 'Starlight' pattern. Although the fashion for moulded glass novelties did not continue much into the twentieth century, Greener's factory, under the new ownership of Jobling and Co., later achieved success as the makers of the heat-resistant glass 'Pyrex'.

Some of Henry Greener & Co.'s glass can be identified by their moulded mark. Like Davidson, they also used an embossed crest of a lion but Greener's lion has no castle and

holds a star rather than an axe. There were many other pressed glass manufacturers in Britain but curiously only one other regularly used its own mark. John Derbyshire's factory at Salford, near Manchester, specialised in moulded glass figurines and animal models, including a range of dogs and lions based on Landseer's famous creations in Trafalgar Square. Figures included a study of Britannia

A moulded glass sugar bowl was an excellent way to celebrate Queen Victoria's Jubilee. Cheap and decorative, these popular models in commemorative pressed glass were made in unbelievable quantities. This example by George Davidson is dated 1887.

Private collection

139

and a fine pair of Punch and Judy. These were made in black glass or else in various single transparent colours including uranium green and yellow. John Derbyshire's mark was an anchor with the initials JD.

Without marks, looking up the registration stamps and embossed patent numbers can identify the work of other smaller British factories. Many registered numbers are given in the specialist books listed at the end of this chapter. Several competent makers were based around Manchester including Birtles, Tate & Co. who produced interesting colours and their own version of 'Pearline'. Nearby Molineaux, Webb & Co. specialised in copies of cut glass patterns and are best known for their pattern of a Greek-key design raised on a semi-frosted background. One little known but very accomplished maker was W.H. Heppell of Newcastle. For the local market Heppell specialised in posy holders shaped as coal trucks and I admire some of their designs for cream jugs shaped as fish or shells that were cast in a brilliant milk white.

In Europe the mass production of pressed

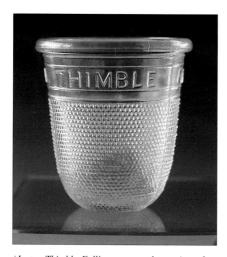

'Just a Thimble Full' was a popular saying when asking for a small measure of liquor. This giant thimble in pressed glass would hold a decent shot of spirit or full glass of sherry, and so made a fun gift to a friend. Northern England, c.1890.

glass was not restricted to Britain. French opaline glass became very commercial early in the twentieth century. Moulded toilet bottles and dishes for dressing tables were given shiny ormolu mounts, and sets of wine goblets were popular in bright turquoise, white or deep blue especially. From the numbers surviving, every French home seems to have owned a pressed glass egg basket in the shape of a chicken. Yet in terms of quantity and variety, America continued to lead the world in moulded glass production and technology.

Alongside moulded glass dishes and novelties, cheap moulded glass oil lamps revolutionised domestic lighting in America. Decorative pressed glass lamps were filled with whale oil and subsequently with kerosene and these burned brighter with new moulded glass chimneys. The production of glass bottles was of far greater importance to the future of the industry. Special bottles were designed for mineral waters, patent medicines and all kinds of alcoholic and soft drinks and their shapes became advertisements. John Landis Mason patented in 1858 an improved domestic preserving jar which enabled families to keep produce longer and more hygienically, and in 1903 Michael Owen's new automatic bottle blowing machine revolutionised factory glassmaking. Moulded glass became so cheap that bottles were no longer returned for refilling. Once empty, glass containers were kept as decoration and a huge collectors' field opened up as a result. Everybody kept coloured glass bottles on a shelf just to look pretty.

Two new developments in pressed glass are firmly associated with the United States, although the origins are not so clear. In the 1860s and '70s Bohemian and English glassmakers had experimented with 'iridescent glass' using chloride of tin and barium nitrate to create metallic lustres on the surface of coloured glass. Thomas Webb perfected 'Bronze Glass' in 1877, although this was blown rather than moulded. Henry Greener & Co. was producing moulded iridescent glass as early as 1880. John Northwood had also made bronze glass in Stourbridge, and his sons Harry and Carl Northwood learnt glassmaking from

The exotic rainbow iridescence on Northwood's 'Carnival Glass' disguises its origin, for the best examples come from the 'Black Country' of the West Midlands. Similar pieces were made in Bohemia and the United States where high prices are paid for rare colours and unusual shapes. c.1890-1920.

their father before emigrating to the United States in 1881. They established several glass-works in Ohio and then Pennsylvania, moving finally to Wheeling, West Virginia in 1902. The Northwood Glass Co. was one of the largest makers of pressed 'Pattern Glass', specialising in tableware imitating cut patterns. The Fenton glassworks in Williamstown is usually credited with originating 'Carnival Glass' ahead of the Northwoods who first made 'Dope Ware' in 1908. Pressed glass was sprayed with solutions of metallic salts and, as it cooled, the distinctive rainbow surface developed.

Iridescent moulded glass was cheap and proved popular as prizes at fairgrounds, hence the name Carnival glass. Several factories in Ohio and Pennsylvania made their own distinctive patterns, including the Fenton, Imperial and Millersburg Glass Companies.

The Northwood Glass Co. seemed to understand the material best of all. They produced some of the most successful designs including 'Grape and Cable' and their famous 'Peacock at the Fountain' patented in 1914. A great deal of American carnival glass was exported to Europe, and copies were made in Czechoslovakia, in Northern Britain and in Australia. Fashions changed, however, and sales of Carnival glass fell sharply after 1915. Today there is a massive collectors' market in Carnival glass, principally in America, with numerous catalogues and price guides available to aid identification. Some rare colours and patterns are surprisingly expensive, but beware of later reproductions, often made using original moulds.

Although Carnival glass fell from favour, pressed glass continued to sell in great

A French moulded glass covered muffin dish from the early 20th century. Lacy designs in old French opaline colours would in due course influence American 'Depression Glass'.

'Rubine', a bright flame red, is one of the more unusual colours from Sowerby's factory, worth ten times as much as the same shape in amber or colourless glass. Marked with the peacock head crest. c.1920.

quantities in America during the 1920s and '30s. Mass-production meant that fruit sets, teasets and even dinner sets in glass were cheaper than porcelain. The taste was for dainty patterns in very pale coloured transparent glass. This became known as 'Depression Glass' because during the Great Depression many homes in America couldn't afford new china sets and settled for services of cheap pressed glass instead. Depression glass has even more collectors than Carnival glass and just as many books are available to assist with identification and suggested values. Production of Depression glass was not restricted to America, however, as related glassware was made in many parts of Europe. In France during the 1920s there was a rebirth in interest in moulded glass thanks to the inspiration of René Lalique whose work is discussed in Chapter 13.

Further reading

Colin Lattimore, *English Nineteenth Century Press-Moulded Glass,* London 1979

Barbara Morris, *Victorian Table Glass and Ornaments,* London 1978

Raymond Slack, *English Pressed Glass 1830-1900,* London 1987

Jane S. Spillman, *American and European Pressed Glass in the Corning Museum of Glass,* New York 1973

A caramel coloured cream jug in pressed glass, c.1890, the shape typically copying a cut glass design of forty years earlier. This example is probably American.

CHAPTER 11

Carved and Engraved Glass

Displays by Continental glass manufacturers at the Great Exhibition showed how far Britain had fallen behind in the area of artistic glassware. In particular English engravers lacked the flair exhibited by craftsmen from Bohemia. Sunderland glass rummers engraved with endless views of the bridge over the Wear were not far removed in spirit from Bohemian tumblers depicting spa resorts, but Britain had nothing to match the

magnificent goblets with stags in woodlands or scenes of Arab horses and riders.

Most independent glass engravers working in England were little more than amateurs such as T. Sutherland who had revived the Dutch technique of diamond-point engraving. British manufacturers and glass dealers realised their shortcomings and invited some of the finest German and Bohemian glass artists to come and work for them. Many emigrated to

A tumbler engraved by T. Sutherland with Florence Nightingale in the hospital at Scutari, commemorating her heroic return from the Crimea and visit to Queen Victoria at Balmoral in 1856. The old Dutch technique of diamond-point engraving was revived by Sutherland who worked in Windsor before moving to Scotland.

Franz Paul Zach excelled at the difficult technique of intaglio engraving. This wheel-engraved vase manages to capture remarkable detail cut through the blue overlay to reveal the colourless glass beneath. c.1860. 12½in. (32cm).

London, Birmingham, Edinburgh and Dublin where they set up their own engraving studios or worked within major glassworks producing exhibition-quality pieces. Engravers like August Bohm really were the best of their profession, and the work they produced in Britain earned greater recognition than they had enjoyed in their homeland. Whole families of glass artists were encouraged to join them, resulting in a transformation of British glass-making talent. By the 1870s England had over-taken Bohemia as home to the world's best engravers, a situation fuelled by the prosperous patrons who bought their costly jugs and decanters.

It is hard to single out individual masters for there were so many magnificent artists at work in Britain and Bohemia and very few were ever permitted to sign their engravings. At the exhibitions the gold medals and the credit mostly went to the china and glass dealers like Apsley Pellatt and Co., J.G. Green and Copeland who employed the craftsmen, although some praise was left for engravers such as Paul Oppitz, Frederick Kny and William Fritsche who were awarded individual medals at some of the same exhibitions.

Kny and Fritsche had both been attracted to join Thomas Webb's glassworks in Stourbridge where the finest quality blank glass was created for them. English lead crystal was completely colourless and free from impurities – a vital factor when carving a single exhibition piece could take more than a year. It is almost impossible to contemplate the task that faced Frederick Kny when he was

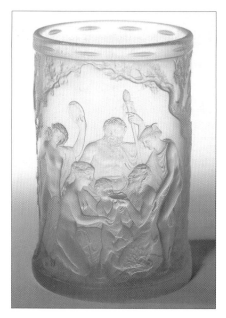

Guiseppe de Giovanni is believed to have trained in Naples carving shell cameos before turning his hand to glass engraving. This exceptional beaker depicting the childhood of Bacchus was carved in England and exhibited in 1878. 5½in. (14cm).

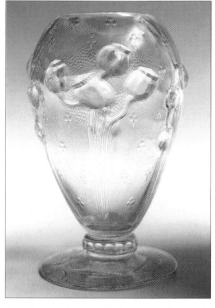

Victorian 'Rock Crystal' glass engraving gently merged into the Art Nouveau movement, for many subtle designs were carved in colourless glass. This vase is unsigned and, without an attribution, at £200 ($300) remarkably inexpensive for the workmanship it represents. c.1900.

A triumph of wheel engraving, the work of Frederick Kny who came to Stourbridge about 1860 and worked for Thomas Webb. This ornamental claret jug depicting Boadicea revives the Renaissance technique of carving rock crystal. c.1870. 12¼in. (32.5cm).

A Webb presentation jug engraved in Australia in January 1884 by Frank Webb who had left Stourbridge to settle in Sydney working as a glass engraver. Australia was a valuable export market for European manufacturers as little glass was ever manufactured locally. 9⅞in. (25cm).

presented with the plain claret jug shown above (left). The whole thing is just a few millimetres thick and yet, with his tiny copper cutting wheels, Kny was able to slice and polish the surface to create a scene conveying the most amazing depth and detail.

William Fritsche took the art of 'Rock Crystal' carving to a stunning new level of achievement. Named in tribute to the carved mineral masterpieces made during the Renaissance, Webbs' Rock Crystal was, of course, lead glass. It was cut in dramatic three-dimensional forms, a time consuming and very costly process. Webb decanters such as those

shown in the frontispiece cost £36 each in the 1890s, in those days a huge sum by any standards, while the single glasses cost £2 each. The set was made to be used and enjoyed, however, and there was no shortage of customers who wanted the best, especially in America. Fritsche's masterpiece, a jug carved with fish and Neptune's mask, supposedly took him two and a half years to complete. This was exhibited and sold in New York and is now in the Corning Museum of Glass.

British customers favoured clear glass rather than the ruby flashed goblets of Bohemia. Colour was gradually introduced to England

The dramatic shapes and colours of Chinese carved glass from Beijing created great excitement when first exhibited in Europe and America in the late 19th century. This vase in brilliant yellow reproduces imperial pieces made for the Qing emperors, but was instead made for export. c.1880.

Chinese cameo glass relies on strong contrasts between the relief carving and plain backgrounds. While this Beijing vase depicting 'scholars' objects' is in Chinese taste, such pieces were popular with European collectors for decoration in the 1920s. 9¼in. (23.5cm).

and interest in 'overlay' glass led to experiments to revive the ancient art of cameo carving. Remarkable specimens of Roman cameo glass were treasured in museums but the technique had been long forgotten. In the 1870s there was renewed interest also in the arts of Asia and this brought Chinese cameo glass to the attention of the British public.

The methods of making coloured glass had been introduced to China by Jesuits late in the seventeenth century and during the eighteenth century superior enamelled or carved specimens were manufactured within the Imperial Palace for the use of the Emperor and his court.

Plain bottles and bowls representing purity of shape and colour were polished and smoothed by Chinese craftsmen trained in the art of carving jade, and some coloured glass was just as precious. A rich egg-yolk yellow was initially reserved for the Emperor alone, but once examples were made available for export the colour was highly regarded in Europe also. Overlay techniques were used to imitate carved jade, agate and other hardstones, and in some cases a marquetry of different coloured overlays was applied to a single snuffbottle and worked into striking patterns. Clear glass snuff bottles were polished inside and out and the

146

These cameo glass vases simulating ivory with hardstone shibayama *inlay were not made in Beijing but instead were carved at Thomas Webbs' factory in England around 1880 when the fashion for all things 'Japanesque' was at its height. Ivory cameo is rare and can be curiously beautiful.*

interiors were painted by skilled artists using tiny, flexible brushes. Snuff bottles made using layers of different coloured glass were brought back from China as curiosities and these inspired artists in Stourbridge to wonder how the effect had been achieved.

In England there was no shortage of the skill needed to carve cameo glass – the problem lay with creating suitable layered blanks. Since being smashed by a madman in 1845, the celebrated Portland vase had been reconstructed and was put on display once more in the British Museum. The ultimate challenge facing British glassmakers was to produce a perfect copy of this masterpiece. Philip Pargeter, an experienced Stourbridge glassworker, created the first suitable blank aided by a Frenchman, Alphonse Lecheveral who had created cameo vases in the mid-1870s.

The task of carving the Portland vase fell to John Northwood who had proved his abilities by creating rock crystal vases of exceptional workmanship. Northwood shunned the use of copper engraving wheels and carved his

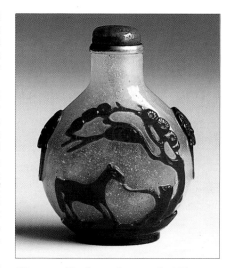

Chinese snuff bottles are the most affordable way to collect cameo glass. Specimens are difficult to date and for this reason it is important to evaluate examples on the quality of their carving. Bottles like this, dating from c.1900, rarely cost more than £100.

'Cupid in Disgrace', one of Webbs' finest cameo plaques carved by George Woodall in 1892. Words cannot begin to describe the incredible detail Woodall was able to achieve by polishing away only a few millimetres of overlaying glass.

A Thomas Webb vase of quite superb quality. The flowing design and the delicacy of the carving are both breathtaking in their way, but perhaps the most remarkable feature of this vase is how thinly it was blown, for it weighs surprisingly little. c.1880.

Portland vase with steel tools alone, a task that took three years. Imagine how he must have felt one morning at the British Museum when he unpacked his nearly completed vase to compare with the Roman original. Lifted by warm hands on a cold morning, Northwood's Portland vase cracked into pieces. The cracks were sealed with glue so the work could be finished and, in spite of the damage, the vase was received by the public with exemplary praise when put on display in 1876. Suddenly customers wanted cameo glass and a whole industry grew up in Stourbridge to exploit a seemingly insatiable market.

There is a tendency to refer to all English cameo glass as Webbs, while in reality three factories gave the technique equal attention. Marked pieces by Richardsons and by Stevens and Williams are in no way inferior to the commercial productions of Thomas Webb and Son. I use the term 'commercial' in the sense of large scale production, for at its height in the 1880s something like 150 workmen were engaged in the industry in Stourbridge, producing cameo vases and especially scent bottles. Inevitably the quality of workmanship varied and consequently collectors must look closely at any specimen to see how much detail is cut into the surface. Acid was used to remove the initial layers of the white overlay and hand-work finished off the detail to leave sharply defined petals and leaves. Appreciating English cameo glass requires a knowledge of botany and how flowers and leaves hang on a plant. The skilled workmen made their flowers so real you can almost watch their transparent petals sway in the breeze.

The most popular cameo from Stourbridge

A selection of English cameo glass scent bottles complete with silver tops. These items are almost always ascribed to Webbs, but the other Stourbridge makers – Stevens and Williams and Richardsons – also made fine bottles for perfume. The swan's head scent bottle by Webbs was first cast in a mould and then finely wheel carved to highlight every detail.

used white glass for floral designs on a frosted single colour background. In exceptional cases different colours were overlaid as thin sandwiches of up to five or six layers that produced dramatic shaded effects when expertly carved. Some pieces can look very different. Chinese carved glass inspired direct copies and these were usually fire-polished in the furnace after carving to leave them shiny rather than frosted. I have known several instances where rare Stourbridge cameo glass has been bought inexpensively, mistaken for less valuable Chinese glass. The high value of Oriental ivory in Victorian homes led to copies

in Worcester and other porcelain. Thomas Webb produced an opaque glass the colour of ivory and this was carved with Eastern designs. Heightened with brown staining, Webb's ivory cameo glass looks so convincing it is necessary to pick up a piece to tell it is not real ivory and made of glass instead.

All Stourbridge cameo is wondrous in its own way, but the work of two craftsmen took the art form to a further dimension. Brothers Thomas and George Woodall were trained locally and spent long careers at Webbs working on Rock Crystal and commercial cameo including fine floral patterns and ivory.

Beneath the skilful tools of Thomas and George Woodall, the dress of Flora has become truly transparent, leaving little to the imagination. The Woodalls' supreme reputation is totally deserved, for no other artists have ever been able to accomplish such delicacy. c.1890.

were never profitable and pieces often took several years to find buyers at discounted prices. Today single pieces can command up to £50,000 ($80,000) and most glass collectors can only dream of ownership.

In the 1870s John Northwood produced some intaglio carving of mushrooms or orchids carved with an unusual degree of freedom. The Woodalls also worked on a few special pieces where subtle shading of colours and an asymmetry of composition broke away totally from the more static Victorian styles all around them. The British public failed to appreciate the novelty and these avant-garde designs proved very hard to sell. They were noticed, however, by French and American glassmakers and what could have become a great British artistic tradition was lost before it began. By 1900 English cameo was old-fashioned and any remaining stock was sold off cheaply. French Art Nouveau had taken over.

Further reading

Ray and Lee Grover, *English Cameo Glass,* New York 1979

Charles Hajdamach, *British Glass 1800-1914,* Woodbridge 1991

Barbara Morris, *Victorian Table Glass and Ornaments,* London 1978

Hugh Wakefield, *Nineteenth Century British Glass,* London 1982

They achieved fame for their figure subjects which can be quite simply breathtaking. Not content with merely copying Roman cameo subjects, the Woodalls took Victorian themes and created totally original figural compositions remarkable for their detail and depth of perspective. When George Woodall carved a lady, her transparent silk diaphanous dress clung to her body in a way that left nothing to the imagination. In keeping with the time, the erotic undertones were subtle, not vulgar. The Woodalls' art commanded incredible sums in the 1890s but, considering the time they took to create, their masterpieces

The neat signature of George Woodall, from a Webbs cameo vase.

CHAPTER 12

The Spirit of Art Nouveau

Japanese art, displayed in major European exhibitions from the 1860s, is generally credited with inspiring the Art Nouveau movement, but it is very hard to point to a single influence. Victorian taste had grown out of control. In architecture and every area of design it almost seemed as if there was a competition to see who could squeeze the most ornament possible into a single design and then to add some more. Plain oriental artefacts were certainly different and appealed to a connoisseur market.

The pieces below are both by the same designer. One owes its origin to Dr Christopher Dresser's love of plant forms, the other his insistence that a good design must suit its

Christopher Dresser designed a plated claret jug using plain straight lines and simple colourless glass. The remarkable feature is the date, for this very modern looking object was made in 1885. The mounts by Elkington & Co. 9½in. (24cm).

James Couper & Son's 'Clutha' glass placed Britain in the forefront of modern art glass, for in the 1880s it was revolutionary. Once again the genius behind the design was Dr Christopher Dresser. 20in. (51cm).

A supreme example of English Arts and Crafts design by Charles Robert Ashbee for the Guild of Handicrafts Ltd., produced in 1904. The plain shaped green glass bottle, made by Whitefriars, is in total harmony with the flowing silver mounts. 8⅝in. (22cm).

function. They couldn't be more different. The claret jug is industrial, using clean lines and a symmetry suited to the silversmith as well as the maker of cut glass. Shape here is everything, with very little actual ornament. The 'Clutha' vase is also all about shape – abstract and individual. It's a step back in time, emphasising impurities of colour and irregularities in shape to mirror maybe the appearance of something ancient and handmade.

It is the very essence of the Arts and Crafts movement of which the bottle opposite is a classic example. This is supposedly mediaeval and, true to the teachings of Ruskin and Morris, it is made by hand, not by machine. Handmade craftsmanship was indeed a reaction against the mass-production of industrial artefacts typified by pressed glass dishes made for everyday use. Dresser believed that even factory-made objects should still be well designed, but most Arts and Crafts glass was anything but cheap. Whitefriars glass, copying centuries old hand-blown Venetian glass was sold in London galleries and in price was quite out of reach of the working classes who continued to use moulded tumblers. Customers who bought Clutha glass, or Stevens and Williams' 'Silveria' that was not dissimilar, would have hated the fussy precision of Stourbridge cameo glass.

In England the Aesthetic Movement went hand in hand with Arts and Crafts and similar moods flowed through France. Yet Paris in the 1890s was so unlike London. The 'Impressionist' painters reflected a different feeling in

Mediaeval stained glass enjoyed a great revival in Victorian Britain, but it was only at the end of the century that designs truly reflected the art of the time. This section from a window is in the Glasgow style of E.A. Taylor and Oscar Paterson, c.1900. 46in. x 18½in. (117cm x 47cm).

Gallé used enamelling in a very different way from other Art Nouveau glassworkers. Here flower blooms, painted and delicately gilded, are hanging mysteriously and almost melt into the underlying acid-etched textured ground. Gallé's signature is strangely stylised too, to emphasise the melted feel of the whole design. 8½in. (21.5cm).

Parisian society where adventurous artisans were appreciated in a way that did not happen in England. In France pottery vases with streaky, crystalline glazes were actively encouraged, while French 'Rock Crystal' glass was based on Japan rather than on Classical Greece or the Renaissance. Cameo glass carvers delighted in the irregular colour effects that Stourbridge makers had found difficult to sell. It was within this mood that an artist colony was established at Nancy. Here freedom of expression reflected an

independent spirit, for Lorraine sought autonomy from the rest of France.

Emil Gallé began his career within his family firm in Nancy, making traditional French glass and reproductions of old faience. While studying philosophy in Germany young Emil observed new methods of glass production, particularly cameo and enamelling, and he became aware of oriental art, the new fashion sweeping Europe. Taking over from his father in 1874, Emil introduced new Japanese designs to the faience works and set up his own Art Glass workshop where he was determined to put totally new ideas into practice. Gallé's glass was refreshingly different, quite unlike anything that had gone before. He wasn't tied down to rigid symmetry and instead experimented with shape and colour to mirror the world of nature with a fluidity John Northwood or George Woodall never conceived.

Gallé combined cameo with other ancient techniques of glassmaking – marquetry inlay, enamelling, mould casting and the use of powdered coloured glass – to create glass that was totally in keeping with the French spirit of Art Nouveau. Named after the modern-art gallery of Siegfried Bing, *La Maison de L'Art Nouveau,* the new style borrowed heavily from Japanese art where flowers played such a special part. In Japan beautiful flowers were not rigid and straight but curved gracefully. An irregular whiplash motif dominates Art Nouveau design. Orchids, not sunflowers, were the order of the day and instead of vases decorated with flowers, the whole vase became the flower with a subtle blending of shape and colour. Gallé had a close relationship with nature, as a philosopher and as a poet, and he saw within the plant world the inspiration for his totally unique glass creations.

Success meant that Gallé was free to indulge his whimsies in creating individual pieces, while his factory produced commercial vases in fair quantity. At its height in 1900 the Gallé factory employed three hundred workmen. High value in Gallé reflects rarity and it is very important to consider how each piece was made. Some basic cameo work used only acid to eat out a

A mould-blown vase by Gallé combines surface embossing and acid-etched cameo work to create a three-dimensional effect of hanging fuchsias. Signed Gallé in cameo. 11¾in. (30cm).

When Emile Gallé produced this vase in 1889 he was experimenting with nature itself and combined several revolutionary glassmaking techniques. The vase is based on the shape of a carnivorous pitcher plant from which could issue live blooms, but it is likely this costly creation would have decorated a cabinet like a treasure formed of carved Rock Crystal. Signed three times including E Gallé fect. Nancy, and Escalier de Cristal Paris. 8¼in. (21cm).

The 'Rose de France', an important Gallé cameo vase using a mixture of techniques to create a fresh and totally original design executed with pride. Signed Gallé. c.1900. 5½in. (14cm).

landscape or plant design. Polishing wheels give more exciting finishes and it is the degree of handwork that determines the value today.

Gallé pioneered 'Blow Out' vases where fruit or flower petals were embossed in a further dimension and, although moulds were used, all Blow Out pieces are rare and far from cheap. Individual creations by Emil Gallé, such as the *Rose de France* vase shown here, are considered masterpieces of glassmaking and naturally command enormous sums. Aside from these, the factory continued to make cameo glass for twenty years after Emil Gallé died in 1904. Some pieces made after the death of the founder of the firm were marked with a star alongside the name of Gallé, but many specimens have since had the star removed to make them seem earlier and thus more valuable.

Emil Gallé inspired other contemporaries and competitors. The Daum brothers, also in Nancy, have frequently been condemned as

A Daum vase using careful painting to emphasise a design lightly enamelled on the surface. The asymmetric flowers and trailing tendrils of the Sweet Pea plant had appealed much to Art Nouveau taste and continued to inspire the Daum factory into the 1920s. Signed Daum Nancy with the cross of Lorraine. 9½in. (24cm).

Japanese woodblock prints of lashing rainstorms probably inspired this Daum cameo 'rain' vase produced around 1910. Very shallow acid etching has been heightened with delicate enamelling. Signed on the base Daum Nancy. 11¾in. (30cm).

much of the Daum cameo glass is subtle and delightful. Daum excelled in a small scale and their miniature vases can be most charming. Daum successfully combined cameo work with enamel painting or realistic colouring formed of powdered glass. Pretty violets, or orchards awash with blossom – even sweeping rain – Daum miniature vases have a special charm and nowadays much appeal for they tend to be expensive. Pieces are usually signed with the family name together with the cross of Lorraine proudly proclaiming their local heritage.

The Muller brothers worked for Gallé before setting up their own glassworks in nearby Lunéville. They produced some impressive large cameo pieces, mostly relying on acid work and rarely as subtle as the Nancy pieces. Established firms such as the St Louis glassworks attempted cameo with reasonable success but they are little known in this field for their pieces were marked 'D'Argental'. Auguste Legras made attractive cameo vases and lamps in Paris, and in Belgium the firm of Val St Lambert added cameo to their wide range of coloured and cut glass. There were many other cameo glassmakers in the same region of France, as well as in Bohemia and in the United States. Some of these can be successful but most are disappointing when placed alongside the masterworks of Gallé. Having pioneered the cameo glass revival in the 1880s, England lost out to France and curiously there is no significant British Art Nouveau cameo glass at all.

High values inevitably led to faking, though convincing imitations of Gallé used to be rare. This changed when manufacturers in the Far East and eastern Europe discovered how to mass-produce cameo glass cheaply and successfully. Since the mid-1990s the quantity and quality of fake Gallé and Daum vases and lamps flooding on to the world market has been astonishing. Today, unless you are experienced, you should never buy Art Nouveau cameo glass except from an established dealer or very reputable auction house, for fakes really are everywhere.

Aside from cameo work, Gallé was not alone in experimenting with internal decor-

mere copyists of Gallé, but this is grossly unfair. Like Gallé, brothers Antonin and Auguste Daum took over their father's general glassworks in Nancy and gave it their own individual character. Daum rarely ventured into the unique and eccentric domain of Gallé's plant vases, but

The metal mounts on this Daum vase continue the plant specimens carved on the cameo surface. Dandelions appear as closed silver buds and transparent carved glass seed spheres against a delicate wheel-cut ground. c.1915.

An assembled harlequin set of drinking glasses attributed to Theresenthal. The designs treat the entire glass as a flower, and invite the drinker to hold the delicate stem as a scented liqueur is sipped from between the petals. c.1905-12. About 6in. (15cm).

A table lamp by Muller Frères using similar cameo techniques to Gallé but with a strong shape in place of subtlety in the cameo design of trailing wallflowers. Signed Muller Frères, Lunéville. c.1920.

ation and original shapes. In the 1920s the French painter Maurice Marinot progressed from making Modernist enamelled glass to creating vases and bottles that were solid like melted lava filled with tiny bubbles or dribbling streaks. His pieces reflect the very essence of the glass furnace and as such they are curiously different.

Interest in an internal texture led to a revival of the ancient Egyptian process of glass paste, melting powdered glass in moulds. 'Pâte de Verre' is a form of original sculpture created by filling clay or metal moulds with different colours of powdered glass that fused together when the mould was heated. Almaric Walter

worked at the Daum factory and created formal animal and figure subjects as paperweights or bookends as well as plaques for jewellery and a range of vases. Gabriel Argy-Rousseau followed soon afterwards and made fine Pâte de Verre vases and ashtrays with applied animals or insects. A further important maker, François Décorchemont, is known for a variation in the technique known as Pâte de Crystal where powdered clear lead glass was added to the mix to give a more transparent, heavier effect. All Pâte de Verre is expensive and so once again there are plenty of fakes about, especially jewellery and pendants. Also, broken pieces can be expertly repaired so be on your guard.

A Pâte de Verre model of an owl created at Daum's glassworks in Nancy by Almaric Walter, an original work of art formed in glass with a magic sculptural feel. 6⅛in. (15.5cm).

The cold colouring of Argy-Rousseau's Pâte de Verre captures the precise mood of this vase as wolves tread cautiously through the arctic snow. Signed G Argy-Rousseau France. 9⅝in. (24.5cm.).

The glass paste pieces showed that glass made in moulds could be individual and did not have to be mass-produced by machines. During the era of Art Deco that followed, moulded glass gained a new significance thanks largely to one man, a jeweller named René Lalique.

Further reading
Noël Daum, *Daum – Mastery of Glass,* Lausanne, 1985
Philippe Garner, *Emile Gallé,* London 1976
Dan Klein and Ward Lloyd (Ed.), *The History of Glass,* London 1984.

This American cameo table lamp uses a curious sense of perspective to illuminate a landscape fantasy that casts an eerie glow when lit by a soft electric bulb. c.1900-1910. 22½in. (57cm).

The dragonfly lamp is one of Tiffany's most celebrated designs and indeed a brilliant concept, the pattern of the wings matched against a background texture studded with bright red cabochons to reflect the brightest light. The shade and the bronze base both marked Tiffany Studios New York. 25½in. (65cm).

CHAPTER 13

Modernism: Secessionist and Art Deco Glass

The two greatest twentieth century glass-makers, Tiffany and Lalique, both began their careers as jewellers. Louis Tiffany's family ran a major jewellery shop in New York but, instead of learning the business from within, Louis chose to travel to Paris for a formal art training. He returned with magnificent ideas and formed a manufacturing company in New York in 1879 responsible for designing interiors furnished in an individual and exotic style. Tiffany gathered around him an excellent team of artists and craftsmen who could manufacture his many totally original designs and ideas. Louis Tiffany understood every aspect of glass technology and encouraged his workmen to experiment as never before. Consequently Tiffany glass managed to embrace just about every kind of manufacturing process and excelled at most of them.

Tiffany achieved widespread acclaim initially for his stained glass windows. These used an enormous range of colours and delicate shading not seen in Victorian church windows. Tiffany Studios from New York were paid a massive accolade in 1895 when they were chosen to install windows at Bing's *Maison de L'Art Nouveau,* the showcase of the latest art in Paris. The success of his pictorial windows allowed Tiffany to expand into other decorative objects. Glass mosaics were used on whole walls or on small pretty boxes, while his stained glass was used to decorate table lamps and hanging chandeliers with brilliant shades that glowed around new electric light-bulbs.

Tiffany travelled around Europe and observed the latest techniques used in glass factories. He was particularly taken by the iridescent metallic finishes applied to moulded glass and some new Art Glass vases made in Bohemia and in England. While visiting Stourbridge Tiffany met Arthur Nash, a worker

at Webbs who was encouraged to go to New York and provide the skill necessary to put Louis Tiffany's new ideas into practice. Tiffany's clever marketing meant that his new iridescent glass was to enjoy the success that evaded Thomas Webb and Sons in this field.

Louis Tiffany and Arthur Nash produced very original Art Nouveau shapes inspired by flowers, especially irregular lilies. The celebrated 'Jack in the Pulpit' vases were named

To Tiffany Studios leaded glass didn't only mean stained glass windows. Tiffany table lamps are all exquisite design statements and hugely expensive as a result. Notice how the bronze bats on the base complement the glass panels set in the shade. Stamped Tiffany Studios, New York. This example was bought from Tiffany in 1895. 18⅞in. (48cm).

Otto Prutscher joined Kolomon Moser to provide designs for glass tableware manufactured in Bohemia by Meyr's Neffe. These highly original stemmed glasses were made as early as 1905, although they are frequently mistaken for much later '30s Art Deco. About 7⅞in. (20cm).

after an American flower although similar shapes had been made several years before in Stourbridge. The name *Favrile,* meaning 'hand-made', was used to sell much of Tiffany's individual glass although there is a great difference between commercial sets of gold coloured drinking glasses and the firm's more luxurious and original creations. The finest Tiffany lamps can now command well over one million dollars although simple Tiffany glassware can be quite reasonably priced. Fakes exist, and collectors need to be particularly careful of the Tiffany name mark added to inferior iridescent art glass. Genuine Tiffany was often marked with the very rough engraved initials L.C.T. (for Louis Comfort Tiffany) and I have seen convincing copies of this mark added to the most unlikely objects.

This very modern looking 'Aquamarine' vase with a paperweight base was made by Tiffany in 1912. The flower inside the solid base is very stylised and as such suits the plain shape very well. Signed L.C. Tiffany favrile.

A Tiffany 'Favrile' vase displaying perfectly controlled 'peacock feather' iridescence, a fine example made to special order and signed in full 'Louis C. Tiffany'. c.1900. (29.5cm).

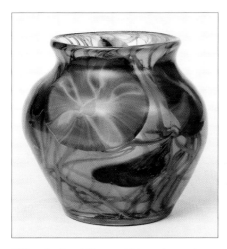

Tiffany developed 'Paperweight vases' – very heavy masses of glass with internal decoration. In the early 1900s these were a wonderfully original concept. This example depicts 'morning glory' flowers and is signed with initials LCT. 5in. (12.7cm).

A large iridescent vase by American maker Steuben in the 'Aurene' range designed by Frederick Carder, the rainbow surface inspired by the iridescence found on ancient glass, c.1905-10.

Like Maurice Marinot, André Thuret produced extraordinary shapes in heavy, solid glass with internal decoration. This 'freeform' vase dates from the 1920s. 11¾in. (30cm).

Just as Tiffany relied on the skills of European glassworkers, other emigrants to America set up rival art studios. Frederick Carder, also from Stourbridge, worked at the Steuben Glassworks and was single-handedly responsible for the most ingenious colour effects and iridescence. Among smaller makers it is worth mentioning also Quetzal Art Glass, renowned for trailed and feather-like patterns in iridescent colours.

Tiffany glass was exported to Europe where imitations were made in Bohemia. The finest Bohemian art glass factory made no secret of its debt to Louis Tiffany, although its products soon found fame in their own right. The Loetz family glassworks made iridescent glass that

The new Austrian design style created by Kolomon Moser for the Wiener Werkstätte was produced in glass at the Loetz factory. Loetz's iridescent glass is indeed worlds apart from Carnival glass. Marked Loetz Austria. c.1905. 11in. (28cm).

The Bohemian glassworks of Pallme König and Meyr's Neffe produced similar iridescent glass to Loetz but rarely achieved the same quality. These Pallme König vases include a 'Jack in the Pulpit' shape that epitomises the era. c.1905-10.

relied on strength of colour and texture for its effect. Mottled silver and gold was splashed on to bronze and purple rainbow backgrounds, on dramatic dimpled shapes with a natural feel. Loetz Art Nouveau glass was not always marked but can be recognised by its quality. Marks cannot always be trusted, though. Another sizeable factory in Bohemia, Pallme König & Habel made iridescent glass with moulded or trailed surface texture, and I have seen several typical Pallme König vases bearing the engraved name mark of Loetz added later to make them more valuable. The German firm of WMF, known for its Art

A Tiffany 'Mosaic glass' plant holder using panels of different coloured glass set into bronze. The iridescent glass of the dragonflies' wings shimmers against the opaque coloured background mosaic. Marked 'Tiffany Studio', 9½in. (24cm) long.

Nouveau metalwork, also produced a full range of iridescent glass in the manner of Tiffany and Loetz.

In Vienna a group of highly influential avant-garde artists set up as a new school of art in order to challenge established ideas of Art Nouveau. The Wiener Werkstätte, formed in 1903, created very striking interiors where furniture and decorative art mirrored the new order of architecture that was dominated by geometric precision. Austrian Art Nouveau, inspired by the Scottish designer Charles Rennie Mackintosh, is generally known as the Secessionist style. The designers were artists, not craftsmen, and they conceived wonderful images on paper. These were sent to the best glass factories where skilled workers created the actual objects, no matter how fragile and experimental they appeared. The Bohemian firms of Lobmeyr, Meyr's Neffe and especially Loetz produced very original pieces to designs by Joseph Hoffmann and Otto Prutscher. The techniques of overlay and cameo cutting were traditional to Bohemia, but the designs were

very much ahead of their time and for this reason they are often mistaken for Art Deco work from twenty years later. Certain Wiener Werkstätte designs continued into the 1920s, when stark shapes by Kolomon Moser were made in solid colours, while Michael Powolny, a very influential designer, created a range of strong shapes in white or orange glass ornamented with black stripes and bands. These were manufactured by Loetz and remained popular throughout the 1930s.

During this period, of course, traditional cut glass continued to be made in Bohemia, America and Britain. Cheap moulded glass copied the old cut glass patterns with very little flair. Pressed glass was deservedly regarded as crude and tasteless, and so it was perhaps odd that a major French jewellery designer should take moulded glass so seriously.

René Lalique's Art Nouveau jewellery earned its creator enormous praise as well as the *Légion d'honneur.* An innovation in some of his jewellery was the inclusion of coloured glass, and from this small beginning he opened

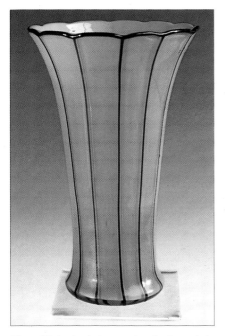

Wiener Werkstätte designs continued to be made by Loetz and others into the 1920s and '30s. This vase follows an earlier design by Michael Powolny but the date of manufacture is uncertain. 8¼in. (21cm).

A frosted glass table lamp by Hettier and Vincent with a typical Art Deco floral design. Such pieces were made commercially and lack the quality of René Lalique, but this still has a dramatic sense of period. c.1930. 14½in. 37cm overall height.

a glass workshop in 1902. Lalique became interested in the process called *cire-perdue* or 'lost wax'. This involved creating an original model for a vase out of wax, carved and shaped by hand and then encased in clay. When fired in a kiln to harden the clay, the wax melted away leaving a mould to be filled with molten glass. The only way to remove the glass vase from its clay cocoon was to destroy the mould, so each Lalique *cire-perdue* vase is a one-off sculpture in solid glass. These pieces were well received and led to important commissions to create individual designs for perfume bottles to sell expensive fragrances for Coty and other fashion houses. These required mass-production and re-usable moulds, and to meet vast orders Lalique opened a factory at Wingen-sur-Moder. Business took off and Lalique was in charge of a huge work-force using cheap moulds to create art objects that were sold through galleries to a luxury market.

Lalique could work to any scale, from tiny perfume bottles to exuberant glass fountains, furniture and architectural panels to decorate trains and ocean liners. His prolific designs epitomised the Art Deco style of the 1920s and '30s. In his glass the mould seams were always well concealed and never unsightly. The detail was always crisp and the fine moulding was often emphasised by applied surface stains. Lalique glass was mostly clear with a slight milky opalescence. The degree of opalescence adds to the value. Coloured glass never sold in large quantities although many colours were made and some coloured pieces can be very expensive today.

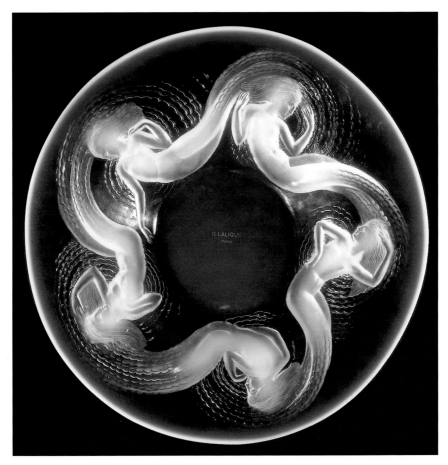

'Coupe Calypso', a Lalique bowl in opalescent glass moulded with mermaids, their tails merging to form swirling waves, with etched mark in the centre R.LALIQUE FRANCE, c.1925. 14¼in. (37cm).

Lalique's growing factory marked virtually every piece of glass, either with his name incorporated in the mould or engraved into the base as a proud signature R Lalique. The Second World War curtailed production and René Lalique died in 1945. The factory continues, however and many original Lalique designs are still produced. Post-war pieces are marked only Lalique without the initial R. All marks have to be examined closely, though, as the addition of Lalique's name to unmarked glass by other makers is not a recent phenomenon. With modern technology superb fakes are created and it is even possible to use radiation to change the colour of genuine old Lalique pieces so that they turn into very rare coloured examples, a fraud that has shocked the collecting world.

Lalique had his contemporary imitators. Some produced just cheap pressed glass copies with little merit except as decoration. Among better names it is worth seeking glass by Marius-

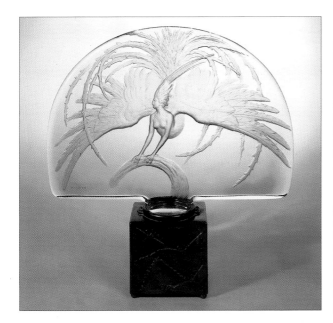

'Oiseau de Feu', a wonderful Lalique table lamp inspired by the Russian tale of the Firebird. Light is provided upwards from the square bronze base and by inserting a red filter the piece glows with fire throughout the spreading wings. Marked R Lalique. 18¾in. (47.5cm) high.

'Victoire', also known as 'Spirit of the Wind', René Lalique's most celebrated car mascot designed to be attached to the top of a car's radiator and lit from within, the glass maiden's hair blown into a geometric flame. Moulded mark R Lalique. 11⅜in. (28.8cm) long.

Ernest Sabino who made charming small figures or animals moulded in a strong milky opaline with a mysterious amber or blue tint. The old factory of Baccarat continued to make high quality moulded glass in France, but mostly followed traditional designs. Art Deco Baccarat is rare, although George Chevalier designed some interesting shapes for the 1925 Paris Exposition. Like Lalique, Baccarat was active in the production of perfume bottles, a rapidly growing market as French fashion houses relied more and more on a unique bottle design to promote their costly fragrances. Perfume bottles – as opposed to pretty scent bottles – are now

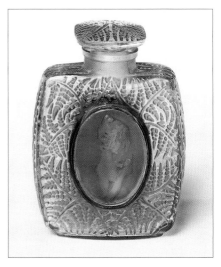

'Sauterelles', a Lalique vase in deep green glass moulded with grasshoppers. Lalique's ceaseless ingenuity allowed him to incorporate any manner of creature into a stylish Art Deco design, 10¾in. (27.5cm).

As the fame of Lalique's moulded glass spread, leading fashion houses begged him to create exclusive designs for perfume bottles. To emphasise the pattern on this 'Fougères' bottle, the moulding has been heightened with green staining. Moulded mark R Lalique. 3⅝in. (9.2cm).

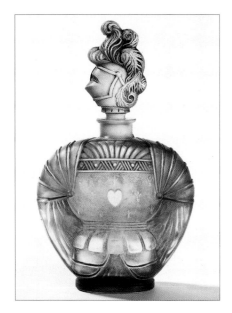

part of a growing collectors' market where original paper labels and cardboard boxes will increase the value enormously.

Art Deco had developed from the ideas of the Secessionists and completely replaced Art Nouveau. Gallé and Tiffany couldn't make the transition. Iridescent glass and flowing plant designs were old-fashioned and stopped selling. The Daum brothers in Nancy were one of very few prominent Art Nouveau makers to survive. To do this they used cameo carving and etching to create modern Art Deco designs, and later still they revived Pâte de Verre to

A French commercial perfume bottle, not manufactured by Lalique but still desirable because the design is unusual and the quality is good. This is Ciro's 'Chevalier de la Nuit' created by Julien Viard in 1923. Moulded perfume bottles can be surprisingly expensive, due to the very large number of collectors worldwide.

Developments in moulding techniques enabled glassmakers to create new novelties. This spray of blown glass tulips comes complete with realistic leaves made from compacted glass fibres. c.1930 and displayed in a contemporary bowl attributed to Loetz.
Sandon collection

make Surrealist shapes designed by Salvador Dali. These are the exceptions. Mostly the prominent makers of Art Deco glass did not continue after the war when a different market called for a totally new kind of glass design.

Further reading

Victor Arwas, *Art Nouveau to Art Deco – the Art of Glass,* Windsor 1996
Dan Klein and Ward Lloyd (Ed.), *The History of Glass,* London 1984
Robert Koch, *Louis C. Tiffany's Glass, Bronzes, Lamps and Metalwork,* New York, 1971
F. Marcilhac, *René Lalique,* Paris 1989
Waltraud Neuwirth, *Glas 1905-1925,* Vienna 1985

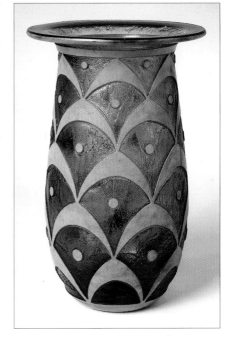

The Daum Brothers' glassworks successfully made the transition from Art Nouveau to Art Deco. This stylish vase of smoky grey glass is overlaid in green and deeply acid-etched with a modern scale pattern. Signed Daum Nancy France, c.1925. 12¼in. (31cm).

CHAPTER 14

Post-War Design and New Glass

Gallé's Nancy school failed because it continued to make the same designs long after public taste had changed. In the competitive world of luxury glass customers only wanted the latest fashion and designs and a quality to match. In England firms like Thomas Webb and Sons and Royal Brierley (formerly Stevens and Williams) remained entrenched in the past and still sold Victorian cut glass patterns in the 1920s and '30s.

In British ceramics during this period the work of independent designers proved vital to factories' success. A few glassmakers realised this and commissioned eminent artists to create a new look. Their skilled workmen could execute the new patterns and these could be marketed using the names of their fashionable

designers – artists such as Paul Nash, Graham Sutherland and John Wadsworth. The artist designer could see beyond the piece of glass itself. Glassmaker John Walsh enjoyed fair success with cut glass vases by Clyne Farquharson in the late 1930s, and Keith Murray designed some wonderful Art Deco pieces for Royal Brierley and Whitefriars. Generally, though, customers in England failed to understand the new look. Examples are now surprisingly rare, but are well worth seeking as the value of good British design is sure to rise.

In Scandinavia the use of artists as designers found much more popular appeal. In 1916, when the owner of the Swedish firm of Orrefors needed new designers, he engaged two artists who had no experience of glassmaking. Edward

An Orrefors 'Ariel' vase designed by Edvin Öhrström and made in 1937. The apparently abstract pattern of bubbles formed within the glass resembles the shape of a seahorse, signed and dated and numbered 27. 'Modern' designs from this period can be surprisingly expensive. 5⅞in. (15cm).

An Orrefors 'Graal' vase designed by Edward Hald, decorated within the glass with a design of fish swimming among weeds. These heavy vases proved enormously popular and were made in large numbers during the '50s and '60s. Etched mark 'Orrefors Sweden Graal'. 6⅞in. (17.5cm).

Vicke Lindstrand, the designer in chief at the Kosta glassworks, instructing master blower Heintze as they create an irregular shaped dish with internal decoration. A publicity photograph taken in 1958.

Hald and Simon Gate used their painters' eyes to imagine new ideas that the factory craftsmen could produce. Working with Edwin Öhmström, Hald and Gate developed a very different rendition of cameo they called *Graal* glass. An outer cameo layer was carved and the piece was further heated, blown and cased in clear glass, so that the carved subject was distorted and softened, appearing trapped within liquid glass. *Ariel* glass used sandblasting to cut deep channels in a glass vase that were filled with air bubbles or inlaid colours to emphasise a very stylised pattern. More recently the Ariel and Graal techniques have been used to great effect by Ingeborg Lundin and Sven Palmqvist who developed the *Ravenna* range of internally decorated glass where brightly coloured shapes were inlaid into air pockets.

Vicke Lindstrand joined Orrefors' growing team of glass artists in 1928 and became their most important designer. His 'Pearl Fisherman' series of engraved vases brought rock

A Stuart bowl designed by Graham Sutherland, etched mark with designer's name. 6⅞in. (17.5cm) high. During the 1930s many eminent British artists provided designs for domestic and ornamental glass, including Paul Nash and Keith Murray. Examples are rare and expensive.

Four pieces of Orrefors glass; the central vase, titled 'The Pearl Diver', is designed by Vicke Lindstrand and the internally decorated 'Ariel' vase is by Ingeborg Lundin; the other engraved vase and the bowl have engraved figures by Simon Gate, 1950s and '60s.

crystal style engraving into the modern world and was highly acclaimed. Lindstrand left Orrefors in 1941 and in the '50s became chief designer at the Kosta Boda glassworks also in Sweden. Here he developed elegant modern vase shapes relying for their decoration on very simple engraved figures or plants, or in the case of the 'Dark Magic' series a single coloured spiral or streak within otherwise clear glass. During the 1950s Swedish art glass spawned a new approach to glass throughout Scandinavia and also many other countries.

In Finland, Tapio Wirkkala produced in the late 1940s exciting plant- and fungus-form vases with finely engraved lines and other surface textures. These were made at the Iittala glassworks where in the 1960s the 'Finlandia' range of glass was produced, cast in carved wooden moulds and textured like cold ice. Also at Iittala, Timo Sarpeneva won international praise for his thick bubble shapes that were stark but meaningful.

In Czechoslovakia the old Bohemian style of engraving was updated in the work of Jaroslav Horejc whose carved figures combined the past with the modern world. This was taken a stage further in the 1950s when René Roubicec carved exciting three-dimensional figurative vases. In Holland at the old glassworks in Leerdam the 'Unica' range of glass vases was introduced, the name suggesting one-off sculptural forms. The work of Andries Dirk Copier is of particular note for its abstract internal texture.

In Britain the most original art glass of the 1920s and '30s was made in Perth, Scotland at John Moncrieff's small glassworks. Moncrieff's wife collaborated with a Spanish emigrant, Salvador Ysart, to create the 'Monart' range of unique blown vases with internal textures and swirling colours. Paul Ysart, who is best known for his paperweights, worked on the Monart pieces and also on the similar 'Vasart' range.

In the post-war period originality in English glass was generally lacking. The most important artist in British glass was Laurence

Whitefriars glass from the 1960s and '70s, designed by Geoffrey Baxter in a variety of original textures including treebark effect. Originally very inexpensive and now highly collectable.

A collection of British 1930s Art Glass vases. Top left: James Powell, Whitefriars, and bottom centre: Gray-Stan. The other three are Monart in typically Scottish style with internal decoration including gold flecks. 10¼in-11in. (26-28cm).

Whistler who in 1935 revived the old techniques of diamond-point engraving and calligraphy to illustrate poetry with a subtlety that has never been equalled. Other artists took up the technique including John Hutton who created engraved screens for Coventry and other cathedrals and produced a series of large vases made at Webbs.

In the 1960s England began to rival Scandinavia with the thick-walled vases made at Whitefriars to designs by Geoffrey Baxter. Blown into textured moulds, these geometric forms glow with vibrant colours and, after two decades of neglect, are now keenly collected. The Wedgwood ceramic factory opened a glass studio producing some original designs by Robert Stennett-Wilson and a range of paper-weight animals that have charm as inexpensive novelties, but the studio initiative was slow to take off in England. Instead, in modern design and studio glass, Italy and the United States took the lead.

The greatest name in modern Italian glass is that of Paulo Venini. His career began in Murano making reproductions of old Venetian drinking glasses and *latticinio* patterns. In the 1920s he set up on his own as a studio glassmaker with dreams of producing some-thing very different. In 1932 he appointed Carlo Scarpa as Art Director and began to combine old techniques with new colours, making millefiori and mosaic glass in original shapes. After the war, Venini's wife Ginette Ginous encouraged even brighter colours and the new Venini palette was born.

In 1947 Fulvio Bianconi joined Venini, bringing humour and fresh originality to his designs. Bianconi was responsible for the famous Venini handkerchief vases. A square of patterned glass was heated and draped over a post and allowed to fold naturally and cool in the shape of a bowl or vase that looked just like a coloured silk handkerchief. Many were made

A dramatic 1950s Venini bottle shaped vase designed by Carlo Scarpa, signed 'Venini ltalia.' 18⅛in. (46cm).

A Venini Pezzati *vase by Fulvio Bianconi, a prolific and very influential designer. This characteristic shape is decorated with a patchwork pattern in different colours, stamped Venini Murano Italia. 6¾in. (17cm).*

in *latticinio* and filigree like Venetian of old, while others were in the new colours. Paulo Venini and Bianconi created *Pezzati* vases where blocks of different colours were fused together like patchwork. Other patterns were woven together out of strips of coloured glass. Tall bottles, known as *Morandi* were made from concentric bands of primary colours and these were seen as sculptural art objects, not decanters for liqueur.

Without function, Venini ornaments became more outrageous. Tobia Scarpa created *Occhi* vases looking like nets of bright single colours enclosing clear glass windows or 'eyes'. In the mid-1950s Paulo Venini designed shapes of stacked cones or linked bubbles of different colours. Vases took the shape of fish or crazy animals and figure ornaments were made of characters from the old *Commedia dell'arte* but brought bang up to date. Venini

A large Murano glass sculpture by Lorendano Rosin, one of many talented designers who follow the traditions of Venini and Barovier, signed with paper label, 1970s. 38½in. (98cm).

Italian Designer Glass from the 1950s and '60s, including, from left, a bowl by Tobia Scarpa, a decanter by Archimede Seguso, a vase by Thomas Stearns, and right, an egg and a vase by Ludovico Santillana flanking a vase by Tony Zuccheri. The glass turkey is also by Venini. 14in. (35.5cm).

A Venini 'Handkerchief Vase', a very simple idea created by Fulvio Bianconi and produced in quantities during the 1950s and early '60s. This small example in vetro à fili is signed Venini Murano Italia. 4in. (10cm) high.

glass won prizes in exhibitions all round the world and inspired many followers. There were, of course many other glass firms in Venice and most realised fashion had changed and they needed new designers.

Ercole Barovier ran the family firm of Barovier and Toso. He produced copies of Venini's *Pezzati* glass but generally in softer colours. Barovier was responsible for many original creations, especially glass with a primitive or corroded finish to which he gave names like *Neolitico* and *Aborigino*. Flavio Poli was Art Director at the firm of Seguso Vetri d'Arte where biomorphic shaped sculptures were made clearly influenced by Scandinavian glass. Some of these were made by Archimede Seguso who also applied carefully controlled lace patterns to the surface of coloured glass. Venetian glass became more and more international. The Finnish glass-

A range of humorous glass figures and animals including examples from Venice and Czechoslovakia. Very few of these items could be considered great works of great art, but collecting such novelties is great fun and generally inexpensive. 1950s-'80s.

maker Tapio Wirkkala and leading American glass artist Dale Chihuly were among many artists who came to Murano both to learn and to instruct. In addition great names like Picasso, Chagall and Alexander Calder allowed their designs to be copied in glass at various Murano factories. Today Venice remains a major centre for originality in modern glass.

Although Tiffany and other original glassworks failed to survive the depression years in America, fresh ideas continued at Steuben. Taking its lead from England, the commercial glass factory commissioned major artists around the world to produce designs that could be copied by their engravers. Jean Cocteau, Marie Laurencin, Georgia O'Keefe – the list encompasses some of the greatest names in twentieth century art. Although the images were merely copies, the names alone brought fame to Steuben and helped sell their free-form vases and sculpture.

Nearby in Corning the industrial glass factory encouraged study by forming a collection of the great glass of the past, rivalling the fine collection of ancient glass at the Toledo Museum of Art. As well as bolstering the study of ancient glass, these two great museums supported modern glass by sponsoring exhibitions and awarding prizes to studio artists. A whole new Studio Glass movement was born out of this collaboration between museums, universities and art colleges across America. Harvey Littleton, who had been inspired by Andries Copier's work at Leerdam, set up a studio at the University of Wisconsin where he made very original freeform sculptures balancing contrasting shapes in coloured glass. There are so many great talents in modern American glass. Marvin Lipofsky's abstract vases from the 1960s and '70s now hold pride of place in galleries of contemporary art, for glass has become an art form. Edris Eckhardt trained as a sculptor at Cleveland Institute of Art and from the 1950s worked on multiple layered

A contemporary vase by Siddy Langley, with internal decoration of rune-like figures, c.1990. 9⅞in. (25cm).

glass with surface iridescence, creating within his paperweights a mystical effect reminiscent of nineteenth century Lithyalin. Dale Chihuly is perhaps the best known of the contemporary American glass artists, placing bowls within bowls, each with the internal texture of sea urchins or shells.

The studio glass movement spread internationally. Sam Herman, an American artist, set up a glassmaking department at the Royal College of Art in London and later went to Australia where he founded a similar glass workshop in Adelaide. Museums are involved in Britain too. Corning Museum's important 1979 exhibition 'New Glass' was shown at the Victoria and Albert Museum in 1981. At the time I was studying glass as a specialist-

cataloguer at Phillips auction rooms and never looked beyond the eighteenth and nineteenth centuries. For me the New Glass exhibition was an eye-opener. I stared longingly at Ann Wärff's cameo glass dishes and realised the artistry of Woodall and Gallé was not dead. Wärff had trained at Kosta Boda and makes multi-layered bowls with dreamlike surreal scenes.

Twenty years ago you were considered brave to buy contemporary glass. How the market has turned around, with pieces by Venini and Barovier worth more today than many magnificent Regency, Victorian and even Art Nouveau creations. The Broadfield House Glass Museum in the West Midlands displays masterpieces of glass from the past but also encourages new glass with scholarships and prizes. As the new millennium starts, interest in traditional and modern glassmaking is as never before. I would like to bet that the names of Susan Nixon and Alistair Malcolm and Louise Williams and Colin Hawkins, winners of the Broadfield House prizes in 1997/98 and 1998/99 will be as well known to future collectors as the best Scandinavian and Italian artists of the 1950s and '60s.

Further reading

Rosa Barovier-Mentasti, *Venetian Glass 1890-1990*, Verona 1992

Geoffrey Beard, *Modern Glass*, London 1968

Marc Heiremans, *Murano-Glass im 20. Jahrhundert*, 1996

Dan Klein, *Glass – a Contemporary Art*, London 1989

Dan Klein and Ward Lloyd (Ed.), *The History of Glass*, London 1984

New Glass, A World Survey: Exhibition at the Corning Museum of Glass and the Victoria and Albert Museum, London, 1982

Ada Polak, *Modern Glass*, London 1962

Selected Bibliography

R. Stennett-Wilson, *Modern Glass,* London 1968

David Battie and Simon Cottle (Ed.), *Sotheby's Concise Encyclopedia of Glass,* London 1991

John Brooks, *Glass,* 1975

Robert Charleston, *Masterpieces of Glass,* Corning Museum of Glass, New York 1980

Mark Cousins, *Twentieth Century Glass,* New York 1989

E.M. Elville, *The Collectors Dictionary of Glass,* 1961/1967

Charles Hajdamach, *British Glass 1800-1914,* Woodbridge 1991

Harden, Tait et al., *Masterpieces of Glass,* British Museum, London 1968

W.B. Honey, *Glass,* Victoria and Albert Museum Handbook, 1946

Dan Klein and Ward Lloyd (Ed.), *The History of Glass,* London 1984

B. Klesse and A. von Saldern, *500 Jahre Glaskunst, Sammlung Biemann,* Zürich, 1978

Reino Liefkes (Ed.), *Glass,* Victoria and Albert Museum, 1997

Jo Marshall, *Glass Source Book,* London 1991

Felice Mehlman, *Phaidon Guide to Glass,* Oxford 1982

Barbara Morris, *Victorian Table Glass and Ornaments,* London 1978

Harold Newman, *An Illustrated Dictionary of Glass,* 1977

Joseph Philippe, *Glass, History and Art,* Liège 1982

Ada Polak, *Glass, Its Makers and Its Public,* London 1975

Hugh Tait (Ed.), *Five Thousand Years of Glass,* London 1991

Hugh Wakefield, *Nineteenth Century British Glass,* London 1982

Geoffrey Wills, *Victorian Glass,* 1976

Chloe Zerwick, *A Short History of Glass,* Corning Museum of Glass 1980

Index

Page numbers in bold refer to illustrations

184